The

# Colonial Angler's Manual

*of*

# Flyfishing & Flytying

by Ken Reinard
*"Ye Olde Colonial Angler of 1770"*

**FOX BOOKS**
Fox Chapel Publishing Co Inc.

Box 7948
Lancaster, PA 17604

© 1995 by Fox Chapel Publishing

Publisher: Alan Giagnocavo
Project Editor: Ayleen Stellhorn
Cover Design: Robert Altland
Front Cover photo: David Ihde
Back Cover photo: John McGrail
Watercolors on cover and throughout this book by: Calvin Laur

**Manufactured in Hong Kong**

ISBN # 1–56523–039–6

To order your copy of this book,
please send check or money order
for cover price plus $2.00 to:
Fox Chapel Book Orders
Box 7948
Lancaster, PA 17604-7948

Try your favorite book supplier first!

*To my loving wife Chris
for being very patient and understanding with my project/obsession*

*And to my children Jennifer and Eric*

# Table of Contents

# Foreword

A complete composite of the colonial angler has, until now, been nonexistent. Early books about these anglers are sketchy, vague, and hard to understand. Few have survived to modern times. It is of little surprise that we have a very poor understanding of these anglers.

What their philosophies and their difficulties were are hard to extract from their writings. There are holes and gaps in their writings leaving too much to speculation. Whether this was by design or circumstance is not clear. What is clear is that to fill in the gaps, one has to follow the instructions in the manner and with the tools and materials available then.

Ken has gone to great lengths to ensure the accuracy and the correctness of his character. He has studied the works of men like Izaak Walton and Charles Cotton. These are the historical registers from which information is available. Ken has examined collections that house surviving samples of 18th century tackle. By exercising only that which can be verified to the 18th century, he has eliminated errors that arise out of using later techniques prematurely. Although some individuals may have been more advanced, I think this is an accurate portrayal of what it was like to be a fisherman at that time.

As you explore the following text you will begin to develop an understanding of the colonial angler. He was very much a fly fisherman. Fishing had already developed into more of a recreation than a utility to gather food. He was learned, had time on his hands, and was generally well-to-do or retired. I for one had never considered the concept of retirement pensions being in existence back then. There is much more to learn here than just the practice of angling.

You will learn how and where the colonial angler got his tackle. You will also learn how he tied his flies and what fly he used at the different times of the year. You may be surprised to find him concerned with things like camouflage and conservation.

You will discover the origin of most of the rules of conduct for flyfishing. By this I mean what we do and why we do it that way. Many of these rules are still in place today. They were quite logical and sensible in those days. Many of these rules were necessities caused by the tackle of the period. One didn't stomp in the water and wade out within easy cast of feeding trout as we do today. Not only because the colonial angler didn't want to spook them, but more because he was probably an older person, unable to tolerate the cold water on his legs. Rubber boots had not been invented yet. Most of us would be more successful if we adhered to many of these rules today.

In flytying, it's often said that there is nothing ever really new. Everything has been done before, it just keeps coming back around. To a large extent, this applies to flyfishing also. With the exception of modern plastics, this is probably true. Many things have not really changed from the 18th century; they were simply refined.

Descendants of the Soldier Palmer can still be bought in any good fly shop; today, we call them Woolly Worms. Some of us still use braided lines, braided leaders, and loop-to-loop connections. Bamboo and wood are still the classic materials with which to build extra-fine flyrods. Fur and feather are still the basic materials used to tie flies. Not because we don't have better materials, but because it's proper. That is the way it's done, and that is what traditions are made of.

Flyfishing and the way it's done has been a slow evolution—a scenario ever changing with the accumulation of the knowledge and understanding. We cling to the traditions of the 18th-century angler. At the same time, we grasp at change in the hopes of gaining some little advantage. Yet we remain much as he was, still unable to fool "a limit" of silly trout.

With all the disadvantages he had from his primitive tackle, the colonial angler seems to have fared rather well. He caught enough to keep his interest, yet never enough to say, "I've done that, I think I'll move on to something else." You would think that with the advantage of modern tackle and the armada of flies we have we could catch more trout than he. This suggests that he was a lot better than we; and we've had 250 years to perfect this game. I think it's time we revisited him to see what we can learn.

*Jack Mickievicz*

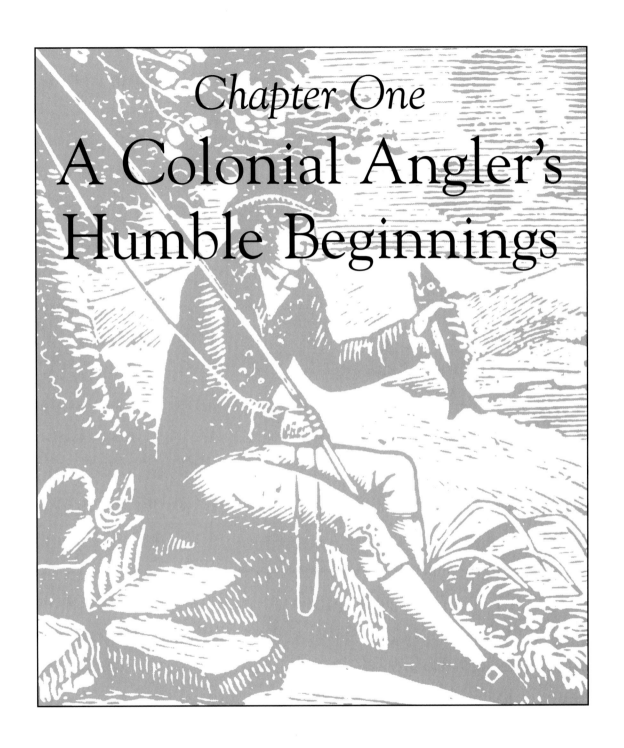

*Chapter One*
# A Colonial Angler's Humble Beginnings

*Fishing in general is the art of catching fish, whether by means of nets, or spears, or of the line and hook.*
*[Fishing] performed by the rod, line and hook for solitary fish is usually termed angling.*

Dobson's Encyclopedia, 1798

I have been asked many times how I started angling, and where I got my the idea to become "Ye Olde Colonial Angler of 1770." My answer is that my interpretation of our angling past started when I was quite young.

Like most avid fisherman, I must give credit to my father for introducing my brother and me to fishing. When we were young boys, my first fishing experience was going for suckers with my father on the Cocalico Creek in south-central Pennsylvania using small red worms for bait.

When Dad felt we were ready, he took us to Hammer Creek, one of the local trout streams. Dad instilled in both of us the proper use of our tackle. He taught us to be courteous to other anglers and to give the next person plenty of room to fish. He also advised us that there were plenty of fish for us and the next person to catch. But the one thing I can still hear him say is, "Be quiet! and don't make too much noise or you will scare the fish away."

Dad always had time to take us fishing and I really appreciated the advice he gave us. That advice helped to make our angling a life-long enjoyment.

Now with two grown kids of my own, I only can hope I instilled in Jennifer and Eric the right way, the proper methods, and the all-important responsibilities of angling.

Just as my father introduced my brother and me to fishing, I started my children out by using live bait when they were small. When they got older, we turned to artificial lures.

After some trying times on the streams and ponds, I started to take them fishing by leaving my tackle at home. This

*A special moment in which memories are made. The author (foreground) spends the day flyfishing with his father along the banks of the Loyalsock Creek, Sullivan County, Pennsylvania.*

way, I could take the kids fishing and help them to learn. They progressed in their sport, and I now have fishing partners. To my enjoyment, they often want to join me on the trout streams with the flyrod to angle in the most proper way.

Our times together on the trout stream remind me of a speaker at a father-and-son banquet some time ago who said, "Fathers make a memory; take your sons fishing. And sons make a memory; take your fathers fishing!" Please note this goes for mothers and daughters, too.

Eventually, as one matures in the sport of angling, he discovers the art of flyfishing and tying his own flies. For me, those discoveries led me to the colonial anglers of the 18th century.

I love American history, especially the American Revolution. I became an active member of the German Regiment, a recreated regiment of the American Revolution, in the mid-1980s. We demonstrate a living historical portrait of the way of life of the 18th-century soldier. This includes demonstrating tactical maneuvers with other units and showing the clothing, equipment, and firearms of the period.

Soon after I joined the regiment, our unit was invited to Colonial Williamsburg, a recreation of an 18th-century community in southern Virginia, to help with an event called Publick Times. This event, held over Labor Day Weekend, brings to life the period when the general court was in session. During this time, meetings of the House of Burgesses were held, traveling merchants visited the town, and the militia demonstrated various activities. The gathering of folk in Williamsburg to attend to their respective business allowed the townspeople to buy and sell a variety of goods. Entertainers added to the festivities, and good food and drink were in abundance.

*The author's daughter, Jennifer, releases a brown trout she caught on one of Pennsylvania's many pristine limestone streams. The brown trout will give sport to another fisherman on another day.*

In our unit we have a diversity of 18th-century talent. When the regiment goes to Publick Times, we must perform our militia duties for Williamsburg, as per requirement and invitation. But the unit also portrays a number of civilian characters as well.

We have Messieur DuBonnet's Dervishers that specialize in 18th-century dancing, a land speculator, a book salesman, a gentleman who raises fighting roosters, a fencing instructor, and Peacock's Puppeteers. One of our newest scenarios is that of two "rat catchers" who will rid the vermin from homes for the right coin. Our unit is also known to play a mean game of town ball, an 18th-century sport.

One peaceful Saturday evening during Publick Times, back in 1988 or so, some of the members of the regiment were sitting by the canal at the Governor's Palace. We were talking about the day's activities and reflecting how nice it was to be at an event as wonderful as Colonial Williamsburg's Publick Times when I heard the splash of a bass taking an

*The Colonial Angler's Manual of Flyfishing and Flytying*

*The author, dressed in his colonial angling attire, is accompanied on the trout stream by his favorite gillie, son Eric. In the tradition of a gillie, Eric stands ready with the net should his father strike a trout while angling the Yellow Breeches near Carlisle, Pennsylvania.*

insect off the surface. Soon the discussion turned to how nice it would be if I had my flyrod and some muddler minnow flies. We would have had some good sport with the bass and bluegill in the pond that night! Of course, modern flyfishing tackle would not be proper to use during an event such as this. Soon the discussion moved on to flyfishing in the 18th century. What type of tackle did they use? Did they even practice flyfishing back then?

This sounds crazy, but being such an avid fisherman and history buff, I had to find out how the colonists fished—flyfished—in the 18th century. When I arrived home after the Williamsburg event, "my obsession," as my wife calls it, started.

As I mentioned before, I have been involved in the sport of flyfishing most of my adult life. Besides being a sport, it is my employment as well. I have been selling fishing equipment since 1976. You might say I keep the boss happy keeping his fishing department well "stocked" with quality fishing tackle. We have a very complete selection of flyfishing equipment and flytying materials in the store. Every spring, we hold basic flytying classes in the shop. I also give private tying lessons and casting instruction when time permits. You can see it was somehow inevitable that my two worlds collide, but never did I envision how this would effect my life.

One day, I was ordering flytying material from Jack Mickieviez, owner and operator of Jack's Tackle and a friend for many years. I mentioned my idea to him, and he laughed a little. But when my order of flytying materials came, Jack sent a copy of Izaak Walton's *The Compleat Angler*. When I opened the book, I found a note from Jack that said, "Here is where you start." So, you might say it is all Jack's fault for getting me hooked on the world of 18th-century angling.

Over the next year and a half, I did some extensive research based on Walton's work. In many of my phone conversations with Jack about

Walton and the other flyfishing legends from the past, Jack would mention the colonial angler, and somehow the name caught on. I decided to research the colonial angler and his methods. By the time our next trip to Publick Times came around, I wanted to be thoroughly prepared to become The Colonial Angler.

So, in 1990 as the German Regiment was preparing for another trip to Colonial Williamsburg's Publick Times, I spoke to the captain of our unit, Gary Myers, about portraying a flyfisherman during Publick Times. I felt this would be a unique civilian interpretation. Gary gave his consent, but said that we needed to get the approval of Colonial Williamsburg first. All of Colonial Williamsburg's characters need to be thoroughly researched in order for the actor to give an authentic interpretation; otherwise the proposals for the characters would not be accepted. I felt with all my research that I was as historically correct as possible. So along with my musket, I packed a ten-foot, two-piece flyrod, two horse-tail flylines, and some of my Soldier Palmer flies.

Larry Spittler, a good friend and member of a British reenactment unit, arranged a time for me to portray The Colonial Angler at Publick Times. Larry held a meeting with Baxter Hartinge, the gentleman who portrays the sheriff, and made some kind of secret deal that would allow me to do the angler but could possibly get me into a lot of trouble. (I had not met Mr. Hartinge before this event. As I had not yet become the Colonial Angler and was still a common person, it was my place to avoid the sheriff at all costs. I was introduced to him before we did the angler scenario at the Pleasure Garden. No doubt

*The author marches with the German regiment at Colonial Williamsburg's Publick Times.*

Mr. Hartinge wanted to meet the person he may end up arresting later that night.)

Later that day, Larry gave me the good news that I could be The Colonial Angler at the Governor's Pleasure Garden Sunday night. When Larry told me this, I was delighted... but I felt a little uneasy. I had no idea what my good friend and the sheriff had cooked up for me. After all, I knew

*The Colonial Angler (right) and his gillie, Gary Myers, stand in front of the Governor's Palace at Colonial Williamsburg, Virginia. The author's interest in history and his love for flyfishing led him to portray the character of The Colonial Angler at a variety of historically based events.*

that no one without an invitation could get into this very private party.

"Now here is the deal," Larry told me. Or should I say, here's the deal he made for me. He said that I could get in to the Pleasure Garden to go fishing at the canal. But, if the sheriff found me angling there, I could be arrested, dragged away in leg-irons, and placed in the stocks, if the sheriff saw fit. Warily, I agreed to the rules set before me. Despite the danger, it could be fun and maybe it would turn out very interestingly. Little did I know that this true story would be my induction to becoming a proper colonial angler of 1770.

I was excited, not only because of the angling, but also because of the party. The party at the Governor's Pleasure Garden was a prestigious event. It was quite an honor to be seen there and to mingle with the other 18th-century gentry. Throughout the evening there would be dancing, quality refreshments, puppet shows, and live music. You might say it was the high-class social event of Publick Times.

We all knew that the canal in back of the Governor's Palace held some very nice black bass and some good hand-sized blue gills. Being a common angler, I needed to seek out the hot spot and try by all means possible to fish this most private and excellent fishing place.

I figured I must have help to pull off this adventure. After a brief discussion on the pros and cons of such an adventure, Vince Newcomer, another member of the regiment agreed to be my gillie for the evening. As my gillie, his job would be to help me with my tackle. And if I were to catch a fish, he would unhook and release it. But the most important of his duties that night would be to keep a good eye out for the sheriff.

So we laid out a plan on how to deceive our quarry and the sheriff as well, for if we were not careful and got caught, it could possibly mean spending the night in chains. We both felt the risk was great, but catching (and of course releasing) the fish in the Governor's canal was hard to resist.

In effect, the time of our outing was our only deviation from the true colonial angler of the 18th century. Fishing at night and without the land owner's permission was not proper at all in this gentleman's sport.

Well anyway, our plan was to go Sunday evening to the Pleasure Garden. With all the people about, who would really notice us anyway?

Vince, being a good lad, somehow found new clothing for us, the common people, to wear for the evening. He had borrowed them from other members of our unit. Being anxious to see us both get into hot water with the sheriff, they were eager to help.

We both secured the invitations required to enter the Pleasure Garden; this usually is a sold-out event. But since we volunteered to attend Publick Times for them, there was no problem getting in.

Next came getting my tackle ready. Because I was fishing at night, I chose heavier tackle and larger flies than I would normally use during daylight hours. I picked one of my strongest ten-foot cane flyrods, a good horse-tail flyline of six hairs next to the hook, and a Soldier Palmer fly. I felt the Soldier Palmer would be the most effective that night because of the full moon, and of course, this pattern resembles the red coats of the King's troops.

I took my rod apart and wrapped the flyline about the rod. Under the cover of darkness, the rod would resemble a walking stick. The flies I put into a tin that I hid in my waistcoat pocket. This was enough tackle to take along. We had to travel light. In case we were detected, we wanted to be able to vanish quickly and quietly.

Now we were ready to go to the Governor's Palace to go angling. Oh, I mean attend his "Pleasure Garden."

*The Colonial Angler demonstrates proper dapping techniques at the Governor's Canal in Colonial Williamsburg, Virginia, as his gillie looks on.*

Upon arriving at the Palace we were greeted at the front gate by the sheriff who was checking everyone's invitation. Seeing that everything was in order, he allowed us to enter the Palace grounds, wished us both a good evening of entertainment, and winked.

As my faithful friend and I entered the Palace, we were greeted by His Excellency Lord Norborne Berkeley, Baron de Botetourt, Governor of His Majesty's Colony of Virginia.

Seeing the Palace illuminated at night with candles and seeing all the elegant guests dressed in their finest... It seemed as if time had stopped and we were now really at Williamsburg in September of 1770.

At the end of the receiving line was the groundskeeper. He asked us what we were up to. He thought that my walking stick looked like a fishing rod and asked us if we were going to fish the canal tonight. After I assured him that I had no intentions of doing such an unsporting thing as that, he wished us a good night.

So far our plan was working. We mingled with the guests a bit. After some cake and refreshment, we slipped into the shadows of the evening.

As we walked down the path in the garden, planning our next step, we stopped dead in our tracks. Ahead of us were three of the finest of the king's troops on guard to the entrance of the canal.

We had some fast thinking to do. As we approached the guards, we were cautious, for we did not want to appear too suspicious. Upon greeting them, we chatted for a few minutes and commented on what a fine job the King of England was doing sending his troops here to protect his colonies from danger.

After our brief conversation they seemed to be more at ease. Being a warm evening, I suggested that if they wanted to go to the party for some cool, liquid refreshment, Vince and I would watch this post until they returned.

Upon hearing this, one of the soldiers caught a glimpse of my flyrod/walking stick. It seemed that he sensed something was up. Surprisingly, the officer agreed that a cool drink was a good idea and the three left.

*The author, posing as the Colonial Angler, stands by the canal at Colonial Williamsburg with his gillie Dan Fisher (right) and Gary Myers, captain of the German Regiment.*

Now, no British soldier would ever leave his post. Could they have been tipped off and knew what to do?

Of course, we were not going to wait around and see. After the guards went around the corner and disappeared into the night, Vince and I left the area. We followed the secluded path through the trees that led to the canal area.

The Williamsburg people had lit torches around the canal for the evening. What a sight to behold! This was a beautiful night, and again, it looked as if time had stood still. Upon seeing all this splendor, I almost forgot the angling we were supposed to be doing.

Finding a secluded section of the canal, Vince helped me get the tackle ready. We met a couple strolling about the path around the canal and wished them well as good gentleman should have.

Then Vince noticed the sheriff and the three soldiers coming down the path, so we hid from them. They sure looked upset about something, and they had to find the two gentlemen who said they would watch the soldiers' post.

*The Colonial Angler and his gillie stand with the Governor of the King's colonies and a ladyfriend (portrayed by Clip Carson and Gaile Sequin) at Colonial Williamsburg.*

While we were waiting for the sheriff to leave I heard the splash of the fish feeding upon insects. I said to Vince that this looked and sounded like a good spot for us to try. So when the coast was clear, we recovered our tackle, ready to do some serious dapping.

Well, just as my Soldier Palmer hit the water, you guessed it.... The sheriff made an unsuspected appearance. Vince and I were caught in the act. And were we in trouble! The sheriff seemed upset at first about the incident with the soldiers and the fact that it took a little longer to find us. After all, why should he be upset at us? The blame should go to the soldiers; they left their post.

Somehow, I felt that my worst fears were about to come true. I watched as the sheriff reached into his leather haversack and produced two sets of leg irons and handcuffs for us.

Well, you talk about some fast thinking. The moment of truth had arrived. But it is nice to know that I had a good friend with me who was about to be locked up as well.

So I mentioned to the sheriff to be careful with my flyfishing tackle, for I did not want it to be damaged in all the confusion that was about to happen.

While the sheriff examined the flies and the horse-tail flyline, I again explained to him how difficult these items were to make. He asked if I had made all these myself, and I answered that I had. "Well," he said and smiled, putting the leg irons and handcuffs back into their proper place. "I have someone you two must meet tonight." He motioned for us to go over to one of the well-lit sections of the canal area. Obviously, he wanted more people to see us put in leg irons, I thought.

Trusting us as honorable gentlemen, he left us alone to find the person he wanted us to meet. When the sheriff left us, I felt a little better, but we were still wondering whom he meant for us to meet. Were we still going to be arrested? Well, as Vince said to me, there was only one way to find out.

When we arrived at the designated waiting area suggested by the sheriff, we looked around. No one was about. We heard the splash of a feeding fish, and I said to Vince, let's fish. Again, just as I was about to dap my Soldier Palmer upon the water, here comes the sheriff with the soldiers and about six or so other couples dressed in their finest clothing. Among the group were the British officers and also the commander of all the militia units, Jim Daniels.

I thought, 'Oh well, it's time to go now.' But instead of a major dispute on what we were doing, I was introduced by the sheriff, by name, to a gentleman standing to his right. The sheriff said, "Mr. Reinard. I would like you to meet Mr. Carter Burwell. He owns the plantation called Carter's Grove and is one of the most influential and wealthy men in the Virginia Colonies in the 18th century."

Again, I swallowed hard and immediately humbled myself to the mercy of these two fine gentlemen.

After all the other formal introductions were made, the gentlemen who portrays Mr. Burwell (Bill White, an employee of Colonial Williamsburg and one of the organizers of Publick Times in real life) and I had a great, lengthy chat about the gentleman's sport of flyfishing. To my surprise and enjoyment, Mr. White was well versed in *The Compleat Angler*. We had some agreement and, of course, disagreement about the sport.

Then, to my surprise and to our amusement, Mr. White said that we may angle in the canal tonight. He granted us this very special permission with a smile and a very firm hand shake.

The sheriff also granted us permission as well and made mention that we were not poachers now, but angling gentlemen of the 18th century. He then wished us good luck in our evening of angling.

After this nerve-racking encounter with the sheriff and Mr. Burwell, the rest of the British officers and the rest of the gentry came to see my 18th-century fishing tackle as well.

The commander of all the militia units, Jim Daniel, also questioned me on my activities of the evening. He spoke of his method of netting fish. And of course, I strongly objected and disagreed with his un-gentlemanly methods of fishing. I suggested that he should refrain from this activity, for a proper gentleman of his standing and rank in the 18th century should use the proper method of angling. Again, I found out that his comments were another test to see if I was indeed correct in my presentation of the colonial angler.

I do not know if ever I was so delighted to receive this kind of treatment from people that evening. I almost hate to think of what might have happened had I not done my homework and had I not been schooled in Izaak Walton's method of angling.

When everyone was well satisfied with my answers to their questions, the sheriff and his company went back to the Pleasure Garden, for they had other duties to perform for the evening festivities.

After they left, we gathered up the tackle as well as our thoughts. We noticed a lone gentleman walking

*The author at work as "Ye Olde Colonial Angler of 1770."*

toward us down the path. But what I noticed most about this individual was the medallion about his neck. Here comes the land owner himself, His Excellency, the Governor. He had to visit with the anglers in his garden this evening and was pleased with how well things had worked out. After a brief discussion he left us and went back to his other special guests.

Now, of course, I had the approval on being historically correct. This encouraged me to be even more correct in my portrayal of the 18th-century angler. I wanted to find out all I could on this particular subject.

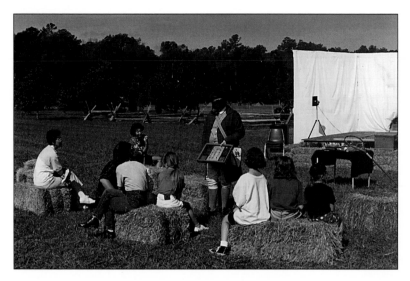

*The Colonial Angler instructs interested students in the art of 18th-century angling.*

Since this 1990 event at Colonial Williamsburg, the scenario of the angler is scheduled for Publick Times as part of the volunteer Discovery Program. Other than the military duty, out of camp activities are termed discoveries. Discoveries are activities that visitors to Williamsburg will find as part of the every day life of the colonists, much as they would have found if they had been walking around Williamsburg 200 years ago. I return to Colonial Williamsburg each year with my unit to portray The Colonial Angler.

Now, more and more people have heard about "Ye Olde Colonial Angler of 1770," as I have officially named myself. I am asked regularly to demonstrate my sport at a variety of historical locations, including Valley Forge, Pennsylvania; Landis Valley Museum, Lancaster, Pennsylvania; and Daniel Boone's Homestead in Birdsboro, Pennsylvania. I am also asked to give presentations at local club meetings and at sportsmen's shows throughout the Mid-Atlantic states.

Recently, my portrayal of The Colonial Angler has been recounted in many newspapers and magazines, including *Pennsylvania Angler* and *Field and Stream*. My techniques have even been featured on several televised outdoor shows.

Upon being asked to write The Colonial Angler's Manual of Flyfishing and Flytying, I felt a little uncertain not knowing how the modern generation of anglers would accept this brief discourse. I hope that some will want to learn of our past angling and tying methods. After all, we are in the 20th century now with all this wonderful space-age tying material and flyline and a new generation of graphite flyrods.

Some think that recreating colonial angling is a step back in our sport. But I feel it is important to learn all about our angling heritage. In that vein, this book is my first endeavor to pull together all the information I've learned about flyfishing in the 18th century. What you'll find here is a reconstruction of the histories and techniques that I researched to form my "school." In one form or another, all the information presented here helped to define my portrayal of The Colonial Angler.

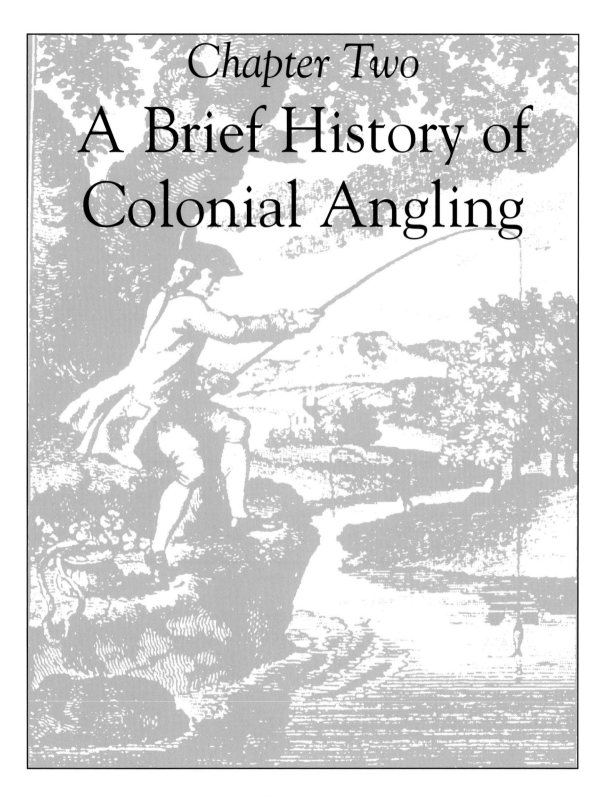

# Chapter Two
# A Brief History of Colonial Angling

*Frontispiece*
*Charles Bowlker's "The Art of Angling"*
*London, 1786*

Many important histories have been written to document our angling heritage. Among them are *The Compleat Angler*, by Izaak Walton; *A Treatyse of Fysshynge with an Angle*, by Dame Juliana Berners; and *The Secrets of Angling*, by John Dennys. In my quest to become The Colonial Angler, I have read these and many more. For you see, in order to be historically accurate about the character I portray, I needed to delve far back into our angling heritage. What you'll read here in this chapter is just a brief summary of a very complex subject.

Please remember that our angling heritage came from England. As the early European settlers explored and settled this new land, they brought with them their customs and their sporting traditions.

Unfortunately, because our early American history was one of great turmoil, the *sport* of angling was pushed aside by the *necessity* of angling. From the late 17th century to the mid-18th century, two great countries, France and England, sent settlers and soldiers to lay claim to the new continent. As history tells us, this was not an easy time for most of the European settlers. They had to clear the land, build homes, survive the elements, and ward off hostile attacks from the French and Indian raiders. The settlers had to protect themselves and their investments.

Because of these circumstances, angling quickly became not a recreational sport as it had been in England, but a means of survival. To survive, the settlers needed large quantities of food. It became customary for the settlers in this new world to fish as they saw fit. Netting fish and trapping fish were all common practices to gain mass quantities of fish.

One of the first accounts of angling—flyfishing, not bait-fishing or the netting or trapping of fish—was recorded in colonial New York. Sir William Johnson was a gentleman angler, born of the Irish sporting gentry. Johnson brought the English traditions here to young America in the mid-1730s. He dapped an artificial fly along the banks of New York's Kenyetto Creek. The accounts list that his instruction in angling was from Izaak Walton and Charles Cotton, the most popular fishing mentors of the time.

*"William Ransted," detail, photo reproduction of original engraved trade card Philadelphia, circa 1770. The Schuylkill Fishing Company of the State in Schuylkill. This trade card of William Ransted, fishing tackle maker and seller, announced the services of one of Edward Pole's major competitors Photo courtesy of The Historical Society of Pennsylvania.*

Johnson's journals claim the brook trout took the artificial fly quite readily, putting Johnson's tackle to the test.

After the close of the French and Indian War in 1760, Sir William Johnson built a lodge near the Sacondaga River for his hunting and fishing convenience. The lodge was called the Fish House. This is where Johnson sought relaxation and recreation with the wild brook trout of this new land.

Around the time of Sir William Johnson's arrival in the colonies in the mid-1730s, the first credited fishing club was started. The Schuylkill Fishing Company, as it is still known today, was founded in Philadelphia, Pennsylvania, by a group of Philadelphia sportsmen. They gathered on the banks of the Schuylkill River on May 1, 1732, and became the founding members of the first fishing and hunting club in America. The club provided recreation for the wealthy of the time period, for they did not have to scratch a living in the colonial forest of Penn Woods. Today, the Schuylkill Fishing Company still practices the tradition of sport fishing passed down from generations of angling heritage.

Several decades after the birth of the Schuylkill Fishing Company, we begin to see artificial flies made not just for personal use, but for sale as well. Edward Pole is credited with selling the first artificial flies. Pole operated a tackle shop on Market Street in Philadelphia in the 1770s. In addition to selling artificial flies, Pole also sold rods of red cedar, dogwood, hickory, and Carolina cane. He also sold flylines of horse hair, paying cash for the coveted white hairs.

At the end of the French and Indian Wars in 1760, the future of angling had a good outlook. Though the settlers still didn't have much time for sporting recreation, the sport was being widely practiced by

*Receipt for General Cadwalader from Edward Pole.*
*Manuscript, Philadelphia, May 27, 1784.*
*The Historical Society of Pennsylvania.*
*This receipt, written on Pole's billhead and dated May 27, 1784, shows fishing items purchased by General John Cadwalader from Pole. Photo courtesy of The Historical Society of Pennsylvania.*

*"Edward Pole."*
*David Tew.*
*Engraved trade card..*
*Philadelphia, circa 1774.*
*The Historical Society of*
*Pennsylvania.*
*This trade card announced the*
*business of Edward Pole,*
*fishing-tackle-maker.*

wealthy loyalists. However, the loyalists, those who pledged their allegiance to the King and England, would soon return to England when the American Revolution started in 1775. Unfortunately, they would take the sport of angling back with them when they left.

Remember, in our history the American Revolution was a very unpopular war with the wealthy. Most hoped that the rebels would be suppressed. But the rebels held out and won the war in 1783. The colonies won their independence from England. And with the winning of the Revolution came an end to the 18th-century angling methods.

America did not witness the return of angling until the mid-1820s. With the American Revolution and the War of 1812 over, peace came to the new nation. And new methods of flyfishing brought a new era to angling.

Flyfishing had made a drastic change for the better. The method of fishing downstream to a rising fish switched to the upstream school as we know it today. The use of the reel, an instrument that the colonial angler used to think of as a poacher's device, has gained acceptance and now everyone is using one. More and more fly patterns are being discovered. New silk line and gut leaders have replaced flylines made from horsetail. Solid wood rods are now being replaced by the popular split-bamboo fly-rod. A whole new chapter of flyfishing is coming of age, bringing forth its own angling heritage.

Of course, my research into the traditions of the colonial angler was far from over. I knew the history of the colonial angler, but now I needed to learn more about his practices.

# Chapter Three
# The Mentors of the Colonial Angler

*You will find angling to be like the virtue of humility, which has a calmness of spirit and a world of other blessings attending upon it.*

Izaak Walton

To learn what it meant to *truly* be an angler of the 18th century, I turned to the most popular mentors of the sport of angling. Their names are Dame Juliana Berners, Charles Cotton, and Izaak Walton. While there are other, lesser known supporters of the proper sport, these three have given me invaluable insight into the 18th-century angler. Together, their works on angling have helped me to form my own "school of angling."

### Dame Juliana Berners

Dame Juliana Berners is something of a mystery. According to legend, she was a nun and noblewoman in 15th-century England. According to fact, she was a writer, compiling information on the sport of hunting during her time period. To that end, she wrote a didactic poem on hunting published in *The Book of St. Albans* in 1486.

A work on fishing during the 15th century, titled *A Treatyse of Fysshynge with an Angle*, is also attributed to Dame Juliana. While it is unclear to historians as to whether she actually penned this work, for my own purposes, I hold her as the author. I feel this text, later translated into modern English and renamed *A Treatise on Fishing with a Hook*, is the basis for most of our flyfishing heritage. Her simple treatise documents the gentleman's sport of flyfishing. I find one of the most interesting parts of her *Treatyse* is her conviction that fishing is the perfect sport.

In his proverbs, Solomon informed us that a fine spirit causes a long and flourishing life. What are the causes and means that induce a man to have a good disposition. Therefore, I shall now select four pleasing amusements, and proper sports, which are hunting, hawking, fishing and fowling.

And the best of these is fishing, because it is a healthy sport. To achieve a long life a man must do three things.

First he must be of a cheerful mind and then he must exercise, but not too outrageously, and third he must keep a moderate diet.

If a man would be ever in a cheerful frame of mind he must have a sunny disposition and avoid all bad company, all brawling places, and all other places that may give one any reason for melancholy.

He should have an occupation that does not cause him to labor too outrageously. He must dedicate himself, to heartsease and happiness, and find an occupation that *demands neither meditation nor brooding, nor worry and are where his heart may find a merry delight.*

*He must avoid all brawling places that cause suffering and illness, for he must go to places which provide fresh air and when hungry, he should eat foods that are nourishing and are easily digested.*

Now to paraphrase Dame Juliana's reasons for stating that fishing is the best sport, I'll begin with her notes on hunting. To her way of thinking, hunting is too laborious. The hunter must ever follow his hounds, laboring and sweating full sorely. He must blow his horn until his lips blister, and when he thinks he is on the scent of a hare, more often than not, he is chasing a hedgehog. Toward evening, he is apt to return home in the rain, foiled, scratched, clothing torn, shoes wet and muddy, feet sore, and possibly a dog lost. With all these annoyances and mishaps, Dame Juliana believed hunting not to be the best of the four mentioned sports.

She states that the sport of hawking is both laborious and annoying. The falconer loses his hawks as often as the huntsman loses his dogs; then both his sport and his pleasure are gone. The falconer calls and whistles until he has become very thirsty. His soaring hawks pay no attention to him. Or when he would have his hawks fly, they sit and bask. Therefore, Dame Juliana felt that hawking also was not the best sport of the four.

To her, the sport of fowling seemed to be utterly foolish. In the morning, the fowler walks in the dew, wet shod, sore, and cold. He usually does not get his dinner until the next day. Like hunting and hawking, she found fowling so laborious and grievous that it too did not induce the merry spirit that brings long life.

Now for a look at what Dame Juliana calls the perfect sport—angling. She claims that, beyond a doubt, the sport that gives a long and happy life must be fishing with a rod and line. The angler has neither cold nor disease, save that which he may cause himself. At most he may lose no more than a hook, or a line—and he has plenty more of these of his own making.

She advises that therefore, his loss is not grievous except the annoyance of a fish escaping after having been hooked. Or he may catch nothing. But this is no problem, for the angler has had a healthy walk, good air, and the scent of the meadow flowers, which will give him a good appetite. He has seen all the wildlife and waterfowl about him, which is far better than all the racket raised by dogs or by the blast of the hunter's horn. The angler must also rise early in the morning, thereby following the old English proverb which states that those who rise early shall be holy, healthy, and full of zeal.

So, following Dame Juliana's reasoning, the sport of angling is a means to induce a man to become glad of spirit and render a long and flourishing life.

Dame Juliana also mentions in her *Treatyse* who shall participate in the sport of angling— "all who are virtuous and of free and gentle birth." This quote suggests that the wealthy gentlemen, or the gentry, of the time period were the ones most suited for the sport of angling.

Looking back to Dame Juliana's time, this statement makes perfect sense. Most of the lower class, or the common people, were too busy trying to survive or make a living to angle properly. It was suggested that the commoner, if he were interested in fishing, simply net his fish. He could also longline them, meaning that he would stretch a long, heavy line threaded with many baited hooks across the river or a stream. In these fashions, he could catch his fish in great numbers in a short period of time.

Now on the other hand, the gentry would have the extra time to engage in this most proper sport of angling. It is obvious from Dame Juliana's writing that a true gentleman would not stoop to the practice of the commoner and use ground bait, or worms, to catch his fish. After all, using flies is the true meaning of sport fishing in which he takes pleasure.

Dame Juliana also addresses in her *Treatyse* the etiquette of the gentleman angler.

*I charge in the name of all noble men not to fish in a poor man's privately owned water, such as his pond, or any other place in which he may keep his fish, unless you have obtained his good will and permission.*

*For if you take his goods away, you rob him, a right shameful deed for any nobel man to do. If he does this practice he is to be considered a thief and a beggar, who are punished for their evil deeds by being captured and hanged by the neck.*

This sounds like strong punishment for a poacher. Well, I guess I should have read this book before I decided to try to fish the Governor's private canal at Colonial Williamsburg. My unlawful actions could have proven to be deadly.

Dame Juliana also states that a gentleman angler must not use the art of angling to increase or save money, but chiefly for the angler's pleasure and to render his body and soul healthy. She advises that a true angler must not be greedy in his catch, so as to take too many fish at one time. These actions would cause him to destroy his sport and that of other men. And once the angler has caught a sufficient number of fish, he must covet no more for the time being. She encourages the angler to busy himself in furthering the sport in every way possible and destroy anything that tends to lower its morale.

> *For all those who act according to this role shall have the blessings of Saint Peter and of God who has redeemed us with his precious blood.*

## Izaak Walton and Charles Cotton

When talking about the flyfishing legends of the past, Izaak Walton and Charles Cotton are often mentioned in one breath. In fact, it was Walton's book *The Compleat Angler*, in which Cotton penned an addition, that gave me my first look at the colonial angler.

*The Compleat Angler* was first published in 1653 and has become one of the best known books about our angling heritage. Walton invited Cotton, his friend and accomplished flyfisherman, to add Part Two to the fifth edition in 1676.

The first edition of the book records a dialogue between two characters, Piscator, or teacher, and Viator, or student, as they discuss angling. Subsequent editions included a third character, Coridon.

Through the discussion of the three anglers, we learn the duties, responsibilities, and sport of the angler. The instructor takes the time and patience to share his knowledge and expertise with the student. The student's obligation is to learn from the instructor and be patient in his lessons. For his part in the schooling, he will learn the pleasure in the art of angling.

> *Chapter IV Second Day*
>
> *PISC: Why then, Sir, to begin methodically, as a master in any art should do; and I will not deny but that I think myself a master in this. I shall divide angling for trout or grayling into these three ways; at the top, at the bottom, and in the middle. Which three ways though they are all of them, as I shall hereafter endeavor to make it appear, in some sort common to both those kinds of fish, yet are they not so generally and absolutely so, but they will necessarily require a distinction, which, in due place, I will also give you.*

*That which we call angling at the top, is with a fly; at the bottom, with a ground-bait; in the middle, with a minnow or ground-bait.*

*Angling at the top is of two sorts; with a quick (live) fly, or with an artificial fly.*

*That we call angling at the bottom is also of two sorts; by the hand, or with a cork or float.*

*That we call angling in the middle is also of two sorts; with a minnow for a trout, or with a ground-bait for a grayling.*

*Of all which several sorts of angling, I will, if you can have the patience to hear me, give the best account I can.*

VIAT. *The trouble will be yours, and mine the pleasure and the obligation: I beseech you therefore to proceed.*

PISC: *Why then, first off fly-fishing.*

### Other Important Works

John Dennys and Thomas Barker, while lesser known than the other three mentors in my "school," nonetheless play an important role in my portrayal of the colonial angler. Cotton and Walton refer to both authors in their work.

*The Secrets of Angling*, written in 1613 by John Dennys, is quoted in several places in this book. His work was organized as a poem and, as the title implies, reveals many practices followed by the angler.

Thomas Barker wrote *The Art of Angling* in 1651. His book, while general in scope, gives a full account of the earliest flyfishing methods.

A final work that merits mention is *The Holy Bible*, for the colonial angler was a pious man. He often looked to *The Holy Bible* for devotional material to provide confidence in his life.

As one reads these words from our past, there is a lot to remember and to learn. These words from the mentors of the proper sport hold true today as well. Maybe even more so. A list of additional sources of information about our angling heritage can be found on page 103.

# Chapter Four
# The Colonial Angler

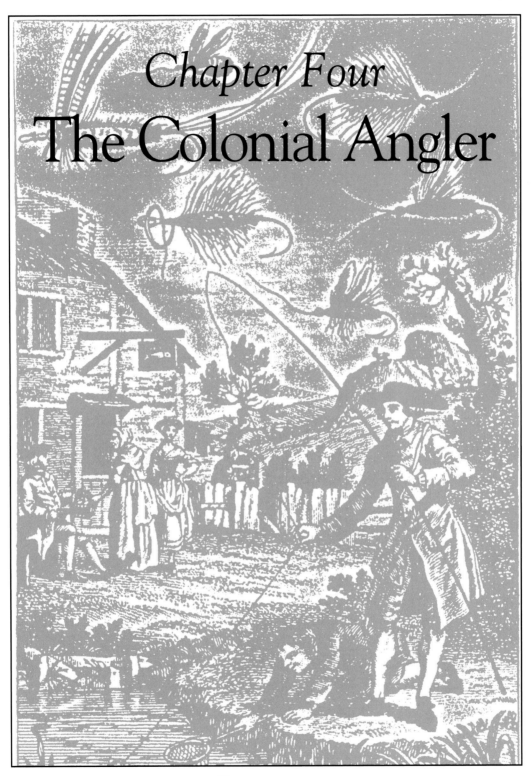

*Frontispiece*
*"The Art of Angling,"*
*Brookes, London, 1770*

### The Colonial Angler's Dress

My search for more information on the colonial angler turned from the written word to illustrations. The woodcut on page 23, showing a

colonial angler hooking a fish, captured the delight of the angler enjoying his sport. It is also a clear illustration of an 18th century angler's dress.

What garment is fittest for the 18th century angler? It couldn't be more different than the dress of today's angler.

In this modern age, most fishermen dress themselves in the oldest, most worn-out clothing they have. Their fishing vests

*Careful research led the author to this reproduction of a colonial angler's attire.*

are laden with every modern convenience—most could fish for years with the amount of material they stuff into every pocket. The fly boxes they carry are filled with every sort of fly possible—many more than the hatch that they are intending to fish.

Some of today's fishermen have shiny gadgets hanging about themselves in order to aid them in their sport. As they walk about, they sound like wandering tankers announcing their presence everywhere they go.

As for the colonial angler, he must follow tradition on how to select his garments. First, his round, fur, felt hat, is very practical and meant to shade his eyes and the back of his neck. His coat is of a sporting style, made from the finest wool and lined with linen according to the fashion of the period. The angler also wears linen knee-length breeches, stockings, and black leather shoes with brass buckles.

To further document how the angler should attire himself we look to

John Dennys *The Secret of Angling*, for he tells of what garment is fittest.

> *And let your garments russet be or gray.*
> *Of colour darke, and hardest to descry:*
> *That with the raine or weather will away,*
> *And least offend the fearefull fishes eye.*
> *For neither skarlet nor rich cloth of ray*
> *Nor colours dipt in fresh Assyrian dye.*
> *Not tender silkes or purple, paule, or golde,*
> *Will serve so well to keepe of wet or cold.*
> > *In this array the Anglers good shall goe unto the brooke,*
> > *To find his wished game.*

Remember also what Walton advised in his book *The Compleat Angler:*

> *By which the shadow of yourself, will be the least offensive to the fish, for the sight of any*
> *shade amazes the fish and spoils your sport of which you must take great care.*

The words of Dennys and Walton are sound advice even today on how one should enjoy his beloved sport. Simplicity is the key. Let your garments not be of some gaudy array. After all, what scares away your sport? What will be the least offensive to the fish's eye?

### The Colonial Angler's Gillie

Many illustrations of the colonial angler include a second person who appears to be aiding the angler in his sport. This fellow, known as a gillie, is doing just that. His sole responsibility is to devotedly assist the angler and make his mentor's angling experience one of great pleasure.

*The colonial angler and his gillie break from their sport to enjoy a meal. Providing the meal is part of the gillie's responsibilities.*

The gillie was bound to the angler by his tradition of loyalty and was expected to do his duties to the best of his abilities. He did not want to bring shame or disgrace to his employer.

*Proper netting techniques, shown here by gillie Larry Spittler, ensure that the angler's sport is not lost.*

For this reason, it was important to choose a person of good manners and of good moral conduct. A person who was lacking in any of the abilities in his duty toward the angler was known as an unfortunate, someone who was not to be trusted.

One of the gillie's most important jobs is to net the fish. Once the fish is netted, it is up to the angler to decide if the fish is to be released or invited to join the angler and the gillie for dinner. Most often, the angler directs his gillie to release the fish unhurt to the stream to give the angler sport again another day.

If the fish is too large or too strong for the angler's tackle, again by tradition, the rod is thrown into the water. The fish will eventually tire from dragging the rod behind and the gillie will wade into the stream or river to retrieve the angler's prize and, of course, his tackle.

Another part of the gillie's duties is to be observant as he helps the angler in his sport. The gillie should be well versed in nature so that he can tell the angler what insects are about the water. He also needs to be aware of the stream's or river's best angling areas and watch carefully for rising trout.

The gillie must also be familiar with all of the angler's equipment. He may give suggestions to the angler on which technique will work the best. He was also instructed in the proper care of all the angler's equipment, including flyline care, care of the many flies the angler carried on any given day, and rod care.

The gillie would also prepare a lunch for the angler and his guests. Often they would eat by the side of the stream or river. The gillie was responsible for making sure that all of the guests were comfortable.

It is obvious from these descriptions that the contemplative man's

*The gillie holds the fish, in this case a pumpkinseed, while the angler removes the Red Palmer from the its mouth.*

recreation not only depended on his own angling abilities, but also on those of his gillie. A faithful gillie would learn from the angler all he could about the proper sport of angling. When he became proficient in the sport and learned all the traditions, he could further the sport and have a respect for all that he had learned.

## The Colonial Angler's Techniques

The techniques of angling in the 18th century were very simple and sporting. The angler was guided by his conscience and a sense of good morals. Instruction is given by Izaak Walton in *The Compleat Angler*.

> *And before you begin to angle, cast to have the wind on your back, and the sun, if it shines, to be before you and to fish down the stream; and carry the point or top of your rod downward, by which means the shadow of yourself, and rod too will be the least offensive to the fish; for the sight of any shade amazes the fish, and spoils your sport, of which you must take great care.*

Based on Walton's instruction, I make two flylines for my flyrods. For example, when I am using my 14-foot rod, I use a horse-tail flyline of at least 10–12 feet in length. This flyline is light enough so that when the wind is blustery and strong, the wind will carry my fly a good 20 feet or so upon the water. When this happens you can dance the fly on the surface of the water and skitter the fly across to the different feeding areas of the trout. This will make your offering to the trout look real.

*The gillie must also be familiar with the angler's equipment. He may be called upon to help the angler choose the proper fly based on the angler's assessment of the stream.*

When there is no wind, I must use a short horse-tail flyline. The line will be half of the length of the rod. By reaching out with the rod, your reach is 14 feet and the fly can be moved about easily on the water by just lightly touching the water's surface with the fly. As you shake the rod lightly, the vibration of the rod tip will be transferred to the fly and the fly will look alive. If you do this correctly, your artificial fly will give you good sport with a willing fish.

*The Colonial Angler's Manual of Flyfishing and Flytying*

*A photo of the colonial angler's equipment shows his creel, his rod and flyline, and musket.*

Walton also mentions that the angler should keep the sun to his back and his shadow off the water. This advice is well worth heeding. Any shadow falling on the water could scare the fish deep into the next pool.

Next Walton suggests that you fish downstream and always keep the rod from spooking your sport by waving it about. In this modern generation of angling, most fishermen insist on fishing upstream. This untimely practice in the 18th century was considered poaching. Only a person of a questionable nature would use this method of angling. It is easy to sneak up on a trout that is facing upstream and blindside the fish like a common thief.

Now, as any gentleman angler knows, one must fish downstream and make it more sporting to a rising fish. The trout lies facing upstream to keep a sharp look out for any helpless insect that is floating downstream as it struggles in the water.

Striking the fish on the colonial angler's rod was quite an accomplishment. He had to keep the fish under the tip of the rod and strike swiftly. If he hesitated when he made the strike, he would either lose his sport, or in some cases, the fish would swallow the fly.

When the fish was hooked soundly, the fight began. Again, the angler needed to keep the fish under the tip of the rod. If the fish moved to the right, the angler moved to the right. If the fish moved to the left, the angler moved to the left. Because of this, the angler picked his angling spot carefully. The bank near the pool he intended to fish had to be free of low-hanging branches and impassable objects.

If the fish pulled straight away from the angler, Walton suggested that the angler show the fish the butt of his rod. This is where the importance of choosing a pliant rod comes into play. Pushing the butt of the rod forward brings the tip of the rod back over the angler's shoulder. The fish was then playing against the soft flexible tip of the angler's rod.

With the help of the gillie, who stood close by during the strike, the fish was netted and then released to provide sport for another day.

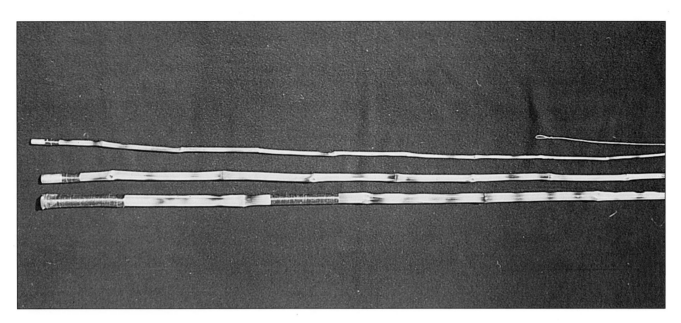

### The Colonial Angler's Equipment

A third aspect of the colonial angler's sport, his equipment, is also illustrated quite well in the wood cut from *The Art of Angling*.

Notice the angler's long, pliant rod. The length of the colonial angler's rod is governed by the breadth of the river at which he chooses to angle. As a common rule, the rod was to be half the length of the stream or river in which the angler planned to fish.

A line, made of braided horse-tail, is affixed to the croppe or tip of the rod and is about as long as the rod. Note that the angler is not using a reel. Angling is a gentleman's sport, so by tradition, there is no need to use such a device to enjoy the art of angling. In fact, during the 18th century, reels were thought of as a poacher's device. A gentleman angler would never consider its use in his sport.

Also note the angler's position on the bank of the stream. The colonial angler usually angled from the shoreline or bank, again by tradition. Why wade where one intends to fish?

Over his right shoulder, the angler carried his dubbing bag. In this bag he carried his materials needed for the day's adventure. He often included his flytying materials, an extra line, extra hooks, a book of flies, and whatever else he deemed important for the day's activities. According to Charles Cotton, "The dubbing bag should contain everything in the world." Of course, Cotton was referring not to the world in general, but whatever the angler needed so that he could tie a fly to "match the hatch

*The rod that I use as "Ye Olde Colonial Angler" is made of cane. This three-section flyrod is 14 feet in length. It is fitted with metal ferrules and wrapped with waxed cotton twine. The croppe section is armed with 12 hairs of horse tail.*

of the day." Remember the angler only had a certain amount of flies to use for a certain month of the year.

Several of the flies an angler might carry with him are illustrated above him in the wood cut from *The Art of Angling*. I have retied them and they are shown here. By a description of these flies illustrated, this could possibly be used in April, May or June.

This brief look at the equipment of the colonial angler directed me in my next course of action. It was time for me to duplicate, by my own hand, the equipment of the colonial angler.

*The Ant Fly was suggested for the month of June, #8. His dressing for this pattern includes the dubbing of brown and red camlet mixed with a light gray feather. And for the month of August, #1, with the dubbing of the black brown hair of a cow and some red wrapped in for the tag of his tail. The wing is dark.*

*Note: Just as ant patterns are important in this modern generation of angling, this suggests that the ant was a popular pattern in the 18th century.*

*This is the first of two palmers illustrated. Again, the use of this styled fly shows how popular the use of this pattern was in the 18th century. I chose to show the Soldier Palmer. In my own angling experience using colonial angling methods, and by modern methods (tied on conventional tying hooks and fished with modern fly tackle), this pattern works very well. In 18th-century terminology, it was a very killing fly.*

Modern day anglers and flytyers are still fascinated by the Green Drake. Cotton suggests this mayfly drake pattern for the month of May, #11, and to use it throughout the early part of June. To tie this fly, Cotton instructs the angler to make the body from the dubbing of camel's hair, bright bear's hair, the soft down that is combed from a hog's bristles, and yellow camlet, mixed together well and ribbed about with green silk. This makes for a beautiful blend of color, like the natural insect.

Cotton suggests using the Dun Cut for the month of May, #8. The dubbing is a bear's dun with a little blue and yellow mixed in. A large dun wing and two horns (antenna) at the head are made of the hairs of a squirrel's tail. In Dame Juliana's Treatyse, the Dun Cut was to be used in the month of June. The body is made of black wool with yellow on either side. The wings are taken off the wings of a buzzard and bounded with black braided hemp. This is an interesting comparison of tying styles and how one interprets the natural insect.

*The Colonial Angler's Manual of Flyfishing and Flytying*

The Great Dun is another style of Palmer-style fly. Again, it shows the value of this type of pattern. Per Cotton's description, this fly is to be used in the month of February, #6. Its body is made with the dun of a bear's hair, and the wings are made of a fine gray feather from near a mallard's tail. The illustration shows a Palmer style, so I chose to dress the pattern with the same body material, but substitute the mallard feather for a black feather tied over all. Taking this liberty from Thomas Barker's description that a Palmer is best used if the weather was dark or a little windy or cloudy.

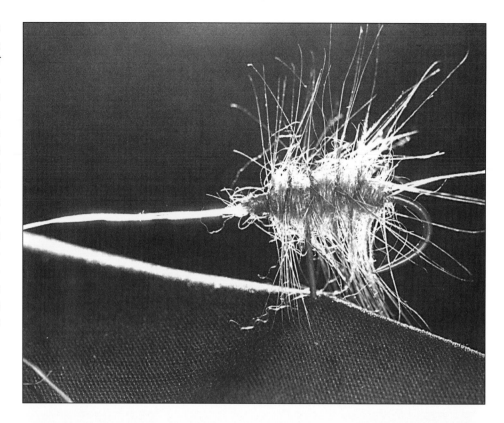

Walton gives us the best description of the Hawthorn. According to his works, it shall be used about the last week in April. The body is made from black ostrich feathers. The wings are made from the feather of a starling's wing. The legs are made of a black cock's hackle. Thomas Barker suggests that this insect could be dressed as a Palmer. The body was made of black ostrich herl with a black hackle wound over all. This fly was also called the Black Palmer.

# Chapter Five
# The Pliant Rod

*And now Scholar!*
*I think it will be time to repair our Angle-rods....”*
Izaak Walton

In my attempt to duplicate the equipment of the colonial angler, I turned first to the flyrod, or angle rod as it is referred to in the books of the colonial angler's time period. For the angle rod is a very important part of the angler's equipment. It must suit his angling needs perfectly if the angler is to enjoy his sport properly.

Each rod in the colonial angler's day was custom made for the angler and the stream he intended to fish. His angle rod had to be the right balance and weight for him—not too heavy or awkward. It had to be the correct length for the stream. If the rod was too short, the fish would be beyond the angler's reach. The rod also had to be built sturdy enough to hold the specific fish that the angler hoped to hook.

Note that when we talk about the angler's flyrod, we use the word rod, not the word pole. Whenever people ask me what kind of pole I use, my reply is: A *pole* is a long piece of wood to which a rope is attached and upon which one's laundry is hung; a *rod* is an instrument of angling.

### Dame Juliana Berners and the Angle Rods of the 15th Century

One of the first descriptions of an angle rod is found in Dame Juliana Berners' *Treatyse*. She gives detailed instructions about where to find the wood for the rod and how to prepare the wood before it can be made into an angle rod.

*And now let me show you here, how to make your rod skillfully.*

*First you must acquire the proper materials for the task of rod building. It is recommended that first, that the buff section, or staff is to be of hazel, willow or ash. The wood should be cut in winter between Michaelmas [into September] and Candlemas [early February]. It's length should be a fathom and a half long [about nine feet], and be the diameter as big and round as a man's upper arm. This wood must be cut evenly and dried in a hot oven. When this is finished, let the wood cool and dry for a month. Then take it and bind it with bird net cord and tie the staff section to a bench.*

*Then take a plumber's wire, that is straight and sharpen it at one end. Now heat the sharpened end in a charcoal fire until it becomes white hot. Burn right through the staff right into the pith until both ends meet. When the center of the staff is hollowed out by burning, shave and taper down the rod to lighten its weight.*

*For finishing the staff, let the rod cool for two days. Leave the rod dry in the chimney smoke on the roof of the house, until it becomes thoroughly dry.*

After the staff has been thoroughly seasoned, Dame Juliana suggests placing a broad ferrule of iron or brass at each end. A spike is fitted at the bottom. The angler would use the spike to hold the rod firmly in the ground. Basically, it served the same purpose as the sand-spike on the fishing rods used by modern surfcasters.

Next Dame Juliana described the lip section, or croppe as it is commonly known. The term croppe is also used to describe the handle or butt of a whip, or a short whip with a looped lash, used in horseback ridding. The croppe was made from two equal sections of wood as long as the staff section. The bottom section was to be made from green hazel. The top section should be made from blackthorn, crab tree, willow, or juniper. The wood should be cut in the same season and must be straight and well dried. Both pieces of wood were then spliced together with metal ferrules.

*The cane rod is armed with horse tail, with a loop on the end and fastened with red silk, as per description from the Treastyse.*

When the croppe section was finished, a double line of six hairs was bound to the tip of the section. The horse tail was wrapped fast with red arming silk. A loop to which the flyline would be attached was made in the end of the line. The angle rod was assembled by placing the croppe section into the staff. The finished rod measured about 18 feet.

## John Dennys and the Angle Rods of the 17th Century

After reading about the fishing rods used by Dame Juliana's counterparts in the 15th century, it is no wonder that future anglers decided to look for an easier way to make flyrods. They also searched for the proper wood to make stronger and lighter rods.

As in all sports, technological advancement places certain material constraints on the inventions of any given time period. In the colonial angler's case, he had to use the methods and materials available to him.

Continuing to follow the evolution of the pliant rod, the next description is from John Dennys *The Secrets of Angling*, published in 1613.

First, when the Sunne beginneth to decline
Southward his course, with his faire Chariot bright,
And passed hath of Heaven the middle line,
That makes of equall length both day and night;
And left behind his backe the dreadfull singe,
Of cruell Centaur, slaine in drunken fight,
      when Beasts do mourne and Birds forsake their song,
      and every creature thinkes the night too long.

And blustring Boreas with his chilling cold,
Unclothed hath the Trees of Sommers greene;
And Woods, and groves are naked to behold,
Of leaves and Branches now dispoyled cleane
So that thier fruitfull stocks they doe unfold,
And lay abroad their off spring to be seene;
      Where anture showes her great increase of kinde
      to such as seeke their tender seeke to finde.

Then goe ino some great Arcadian wood,
Where store of ancient Hazels doe abound;
And seeke amongst their springs and tender brood,
Such shotes as are the straightest, long, and round:
And of them all (store up what you think good)
But fairest choose, the smoothest, and most sound;
      So that they doe not two yeares growth exceed.
      In Shape and beautie like the Belgicke Reed.

These prune and clense of every leafe ands spray,
Yet leave the tender top remaining still:
Then home with them goe beare them safe away,
But perish not the Rine and vtter Pill;
And on some even boarded floore them lay,
Where they may dry and season at their fill:

*And place upon their crooked parts some weight,*
*To presse them downe, and keepe them plaine, and striaght.*

*So shall thou have alwayse in store the best*
*And fittest rods to serve thy turne aright;*
*For not the brittle Cane, not all the rest.*
*I like so well, though it be long and light,*
*Since that the fish are firghted with the least*
*Aspect of any glittering thing or white:*
*Nor doth it by one halfe so well incline*
*As doth the plyant rod to save the line.*

Let's take a closer look at Dennys' description of how to make a flyrod. There are many references to Greek mythology that need further explanation.

First, Dennys mentions the right season to harvest the wood. The first two verses are devoted to this very important subject. The Centaur, which Dennys mentions in the first verse, was a member of a mythical race of creatures of half man and half horse. As legend goes, at the wedding feast of the king of the Lapiths, a drunken centaur attacked the bride. In reprisal the Lapiths attacked and defeated the Centaur. Boreas, in the second verse, was the god of storms and winds in Greek and Roman mythology. Through these two references to Centaur and Boreas, we can see that Dennys is suggesting that the winter months are the best months for cutting wood for flyrods.

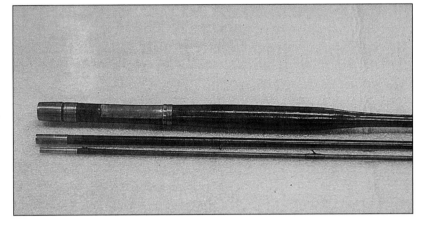

*This is a solid wood flyrod, circa late 1700s. The 10-foot three-piece rod is pieced together with brass. The rod has been stained to a deep, dark blue finish. We believe that later owners fitted the rod with a brass plate to accept a small reel.*

In the third verse, Dennys refers to Arcadian wood. This means Simple Wood, and for rod making, Dennys suggests Hazel. Dennys goes on to further describe the wood for flyrods, writing that the wood must be from a young tree and very straight and smooth.

The fourth verse is devoted to the drying of the wood. Dennys instructs the angler to remove the leaves and branches from the main

*The Colonial Angler's Manual of Flyfishing and Flytying*

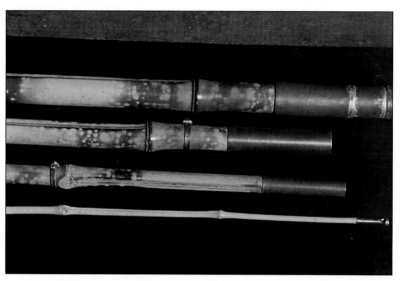

*This photo shows a good example of a burnt-cane rod. Notice the mottled pattern on the rod. This was done by passing the cane over a flame, which tempers the cane to make the rod strong. The ferrules on the rod were made of brass. Some of the first ferrules were simple metal tubes which were fitted over the end of the rod's pieces and then fitted together to assemble the rod.*

trunk and then lay the wood on an even floor to dry. Any bends in the wood can be straightened out during the drying process by placing heavy weights on the wood to force it to dry straight.

The last verse attests to the strength of this proper rod. In it, Dennys also mentions that the rod should not be glittering or white in color or it will scare away the fish. This suggests that the rod should be stained or painted.

To further document the use of certain woods used in rod making we turn to Thomas Barker. His preferred rod was to be made of hazel wood. It was to be twelve feet in length, with a ring of wire in the top of his rod through which to run his flyline. Within two feet of the bottom of the rod, a small hole was made for a winde. The winde, commonly called a reel by modern anglers, would gather up the line or play it out with a turn of the wrist.

Barker's description is the first time we come across mention of a winde. Please note that it was considered unsporting to use a winde at this time. A gentleman would only fish with his line attached to the tip of the rod. Both Walton and Cotton considered a winde a poacher's device and did not use one. Windes were unacceptable by their standards and traditions.

### Izaak Walton and the Angle Rods of the Mid-17th Century

Continuing on the trail of the evolution of the pliant rod, we now look to the description of the rods used in Walton's time, circa 1653. His methods of making flyrods carried into the colonial angler's time of the 18th century.

Walton suggested that a flyrod should be light and made from two pieces of wood. Walton, himself, was said to have preferred a rod of eight to ten feet in length. The best length for a flyline, according to Walton, was half the length of the rod.

From my own angling experience, I've found that having a flyline of that length is desirable in order to keep control of the fly. It allows greater maneuverability and proficiency. The only time to consider the use of a longer line is when a brisk wind is blowing.

Building on Dennys advice about rod color, we can see from Walton's descriptions in *The Compleat Angler* that a painted rod will not scare away the angler's sport. Walton suggests that the best color to paint a rod is green. Using a green color on the flyrod will allow the rod to blend into the angler's surroundings. With this camouflage, the rod will not be as obvious to the fish.

### Charles Cotton and the Angle Rods of the Late 17th Century

The next description of the proper rod is from Charles Cotton circa 1676. In this quote, Cotton discusses the perfect length of the flyrod.

> *For the length of your rod, you are always to be governed by the breadth of the river you shall choose to angle at; and for a trout river, one of five or six yards long is commonly enough; and longer, though never so neatly and artificially made, it ought not to be, if you intend to fish at ease; and if otherwise, where lies the sport?*

Cotton also mentions the proper care and storage methods of flyrods in his discourse. When the angler is finished angling for the season, he should take the rod apart and lay it in a dry place. With these precautions, the rod will be as straight, sound, and as good as the first hour it was made when it is assembled again.

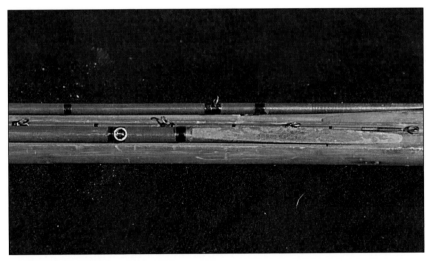

Another method for reconditioning a flyrod is to soak it in oil. This will keep the wood in good condition. When you are ready to use the rod again, take it from the oil bath, let the rod section dry, and reassemble it.

Cotton also gives instruction on splicing the pieces of the rod together. To use his splicing methods, the ends of each section were cut at angles to produce a bevel. When the bevels were matched together, the joint was wrapped with silk or fine thread to produce the splice.

Some anglers preferred their rods to be spliced together in this manner. They felt it gave a better action to the rod. The heavy ferrules of this

*This photo shows an example of a solid wood rod, most likely made of greenhart. The rod was made in the mid-1800s to fish for salmon. Notice the lack of ferrules on the rod. Due to the lack of quality metal ferrules at this time, splicing a rod together was a favored practice.*

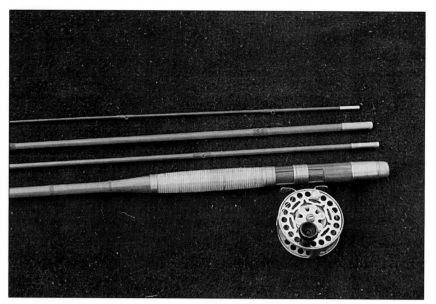

*This is another ingenious way to make a flyrod. The rod is made of solid wood, probably greenhart, and has a stained finish. The guides on this rod are floppy rings wrapped with silk. This indicates that the rod was used with a braided silk line. The ferrules and fittings are made from brass. The most interesting part of this rod is the butt section. It sports a rattan hand grip that is in very good condition. Also, the butt section is hollow, in which the tip section was stored to keep it from becoming broken.*

time often failed causing the sections to come apart.

Storing the assembled rod was also addressed by Cotton. Because assembling rods was often a laborious task, and one which the angler did not want to repeat daily, assembled rods were kept in long wooden boxes by streams, usually near a fish hole, as they were called. Remember, this was a gentleman's sport. The angler could afford a nice cottage along one favorite stream.

An interesting note about Cotton... He is said to have preferred a long rod, for he liked to fish "far and fine." An interesting expression.

## A Discourse of Types of Wood Used for Angle Rods

Though hazel wood was preferred by many anglers, many different types of wood were used for angle rods. We will touch on them briefly in this section.

*Ash.* Used for the staff section. This is a good close-grained wood that is light in weight. It has both the elasticity and strength required for a staff section. Ash is also used in the middle section of the rod.

*Hazel.* A member of the birch family. This wood is used for its strength and flexibility.

*Willow.* A very flexible wood. Willow is easily cut and often used in the tip section.

*Blackthorn.* A thorny shrub that bears purplish and black fruit. It is a hard wood to work with, but very strong.

*Medlar.* A small tree of the rose family. This tree, found in Europe, bears small brown, apple-like fruit.

*Juniper.* A small evergreen shrub.

*Ironwood or hornbeam.* A shrublike tree that grows under beech trees. This is a straight-grained wood, very hard, and very difficult to work with. However, it is a very strong, flexible wood.

*Greenhart.* Used to refer to any wood that was cut when green. In later years, rods were entirely made from this type of wood. The wood was shaved down to its center. This sometimes gave a green tint to a finished rod. Greenhart is usually tough and springy, but quite heavy. A rod of greenhart has a nice finish when polished.

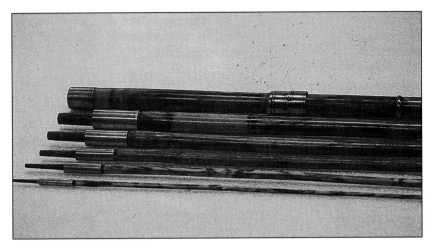

*Cane.* Native or foreign in origin. This is a type of reed that is long and slender. The hollow, jointed stem is very light and flexible.

*Calcutt Bamboo.* Quite possibly the most widely used wood for rod building. Calcutt bamboo is of better quality and stronger than common cane. With this wood, the pliant rod evolves into the truly well-balanced friend of the angler—the split-bamboo flyrod.

The American invention of the split-bamboo flyrod is credited to Samuel Phillippe, a gun smith from Easton, Pennsylvania, in the year 1845. Phillippe was successful in splitting and gluing together strips of bamboo. His rods were usually of three sections. The middle and tip section were made of four-strip bamboo. The butt section was usually made from ash. The rod was then stained to give a good finish to the entire rod.

The split-bamboo fly rod, attributed to Samuel Phillippe (1801-1827), was made entirely out of split bamboo with engraved silver ferrules

*The Centennial Medal 1876 flyrod. This unique flyrod is 12' long, six pieces, and made from Calcutta Cane by A.B. Shipley, Philadelphia, circa 1880. The finish on the rod is extremely smooth, all sections are straight. The burning of the cane added strength to the rod. The rod is fitted with floppy-ring guides and wrapped with silk which means that the rod would use a braided silk fly line.*

*Split Bamboo Flyrod, attributed to Samuel C. Phillippe (1801–1877). Bamboo, engraved silver fittings, mother-of-pearl reel. Easton, Pennsylvania, circa 1850–1877. Gunsmith Samuel C. Phillippe of Easton, Pennsylvania, succeeded in fitting and gluing together four sections of bamboo in such a manner as to produce a lighter and more flexible fishing rod than had been previously constructed.*

fittings. The reel is embellished with mother of pearl inlay. This rod is truly a master work of art for the rod maker and it is also very pleasing to look at. This Phillippe rod is located at the State Museum of Pennsylvania in Harrisburg, Pennsylvania.

The evolution of the pliant rod has continued over the years. Modern flyrods are works of technology. Often they employ materials other than wood, such as graphite—a new, lighter, stronger, and more sensitive material.

# Making An Angle Rod

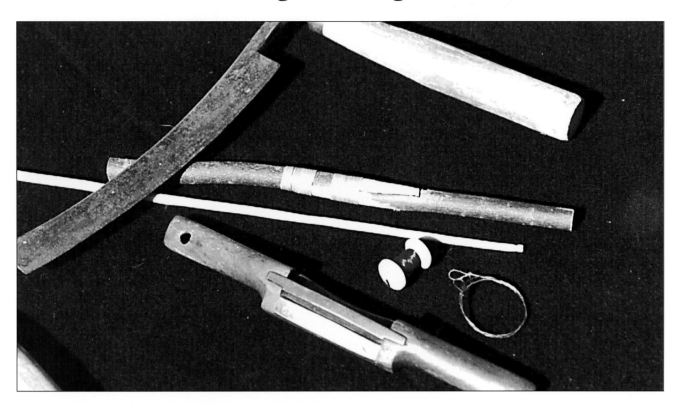

To work the wood, the angler needed a wide variety of tools. Shown here are the tools I use to make duplications of the rods used by the colonial angler. Across the left of the photo is a drawknife. Drawknives are used to take the bark off the wood and shave the staff and butt of the rod. When using a drawknife, always work with the grain of the wood. At the bottom of the photo is a spoke shaver, used to create a smoother finish on the staff and butt sections of the rod and also used to shape the tip. Above the spoke shaver are a spool of red silk and a braided horse-tail line of six hairs. The silk is used to attach the line to the croppe, shown above the spool. The long, thin piece of wood under the croppe is a section of willow. This piece will be used for the tip of the rod.

After they are shaped, the ends of the rod sections are cut at an angle, called a bevel. These angles are formed using a spoke shaver to taper the wood to the shape of the bevel. Creating an angle rod out of several pieces of wood spliced together made the rod more flexible than using just a single piece of wood, as demonstrated with this vintage greenhart salmon rod.

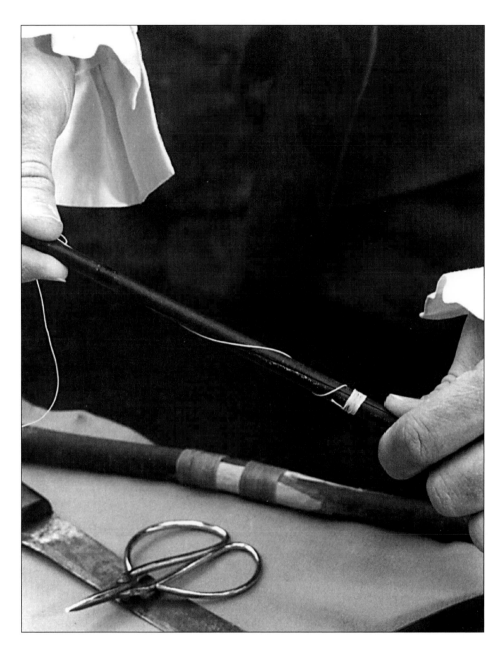

After fitting the sections of the rod together, the colonial angler completed the splice with a fine thread made of silk. The thread is wrapped around the splice neatly to tightly bind the two pieces of wood together. The angler used the same line to fit and splice all the joints together. The rod was left assembled and stored as such throughout the angling season. When the season ended, the angler disassembled his rod and stored the pieces in a box.

When cutting cane for the pliant rod, one must choose the straightest cane with the best taper. Below: This photo shows a skittering rod of burnt cane and its carrying box. The rod features a small, single-action winde to take up a line of braided silk.

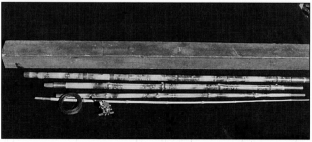

# Chapter Six
# The Horse-tail Flyline

*Let no part of your flyline touch the water, but your fly only;*
*and be still moving your fly upon the water… you yourself*
*being always moving down the stream.*

Izaak Walton

The flyline is the angler's connection to the fish. In modern fly fishing you are casting the flyline and not the fly. The fly simply goes along for the ride. This is the reason we modern anglers must have the correct flyline weight. Without it, we would be unable to cast the fly properly. The monofilament leader gives the correct turn over for the fly. This allows the fly to land properly on the water's surface.

My search for information on the colonial angler's flyline began with Walton's most proper description on how to angle in *The Compleat Angler*.

*…and when you fish with a fly, if it be possible, let no part of your flyline touch the water, but your fly only; and be still moving your fly upon the water… you yourself being always moving down the stream.*

This description told me how the colonial angler fished. He fished downstream and only let the fly, not the flyline, touch the water's surface. But how exactly did the colonial angler make his flylines? What material was used? Again, I found the answer in the verses from John Dennys *The Secrets of Angling*.

*Then get good hayre, so that it be not blacke,*
*Neither of Mare no Gelding let it be,*
*Nor of the tyreling Iade that bears the packe:*
*But of some lusty Horse or Courser free.*
*Whose bushie tayle, upon the ground doth tracke,*
*Like blazing comete that sometimes we see:*
*From out the midst there of the longest take,*
*At leysome best your linkes and lines to make.*

*Then twist them finely, as you think most meet,*
*By skill or practise easie to be found;*
*As doth Arachine with her slender feet;*
*Draw forth her little thread along the ground:*
*But not too hard or shacke, the meane is sweet*
*Least shacke they snarle, or hard they prove unsound.*
*And intermixt with silver, silke, or gold.*
*Then tender hayres, the better so to hold.*

*Then end to end, as falleth to their lot,*
*Let all your linkes in order as they lie*
*Be knit together, with that Fishers knot*
*That will not slip, nor with the wet untie:*
*To leave a Bought or Compasse like an eye,*
 *The linke that holds your hooke to hang upon,*
 *When you thinke good to take it off and on.*

*Which linke must neither be so great no strong,*
*Nor hike of colour as the others were;*
*Seant halfe so big, so that it be as long:*
*Of greyest Hue, and of the soundest Hayre.*
*Least whiles it hangs the liquid waves among*
*The sight thereof, the warie Fish should fear.*
 *And at one end of Loope or Compasse fine,*
 *To fasten to the other of your line.*

The description of the proper material mentioned braided strands of a horse's tail, to be exact white hairs. Dennys suggested that the tail hairs of a stallion's tail were the strongest. Walton instructed in *The Compleat Angler* that the angler should obtain a lock of round, clear, glass-colored hair. The strands of hair should be free of any scabs or galls. Each of the tail hairs should be of the same diameter and stretch to the same length so that they will all have an equal amount of strength.

*The Colonial Angler in search of the proper materials for making a flyline.*

If the angler could not find the specified tail hairs of a stallion, he may use the tail hair of the gelding. The mare's tail hairs were to be avoided, however, because of the plumbing of the animal. Hairs that were urine-stained became weak. Dark hairs were also said to be weaker in strength than white tail hairs.

*The Colonial Angler's Manual of Flyfishing and Flytying*

*This picture shows the beginning and the finished flyline. Notice, you keep the flyline in loose coils, so not to tangle the lines. I usually make 2 to 3 lines per rod and carry extra links so if I break a line I can splice in a section so to save the day if my tackle becomes broken.*

Note that the colonial angler was always on the lookout for the proper animal for the source of his material. As a gentleman angler, he always asked permission of the horse's owner before removing a lock of the horse's tail. He did not simply go and cut off the horse's tail, as some people may think. He always let the owner remove the desired lock. His code required that he be responsible.

I am often asked how much breaking strength, or what pound test, is applied to a single hair? I prefer to answer this question by simply saying that it all depends on the given hair used. As mentioned, certain horse hairs are stronger than others. Different diameters and different lengths of hair will also effect the hair's strength. Also keep in mind that by bundling the hairs together to form the flyline, the line is made stronger than a single hair. All my flylines are braided with three strands of horse hair. The link of flyline closest to the tip of the rod is heavier, either nine, twelve, or fifteen hairs, depending on the fish I'm trying to catch.

In Dame Juliana Berners' *Treatyse*, the author advises that the angler should twist these tail hairs into links and knot the different links to make the correct length flyline for his rod. However, in making horse-tail flyline, I discovered that a twisted line has a tendency to unwind itself. Therefore, I prefer to braid all my flylines and the flyleader.

The leader is an important part of the flyline. I usually use three hairs to braid my leaders. If I'm fishing for bass, I use six hairs to give the leader a little extra strength. The number of hairs used to braid the leader is often referred to as the number of hairs next to the hook.

The length of the flyline depends on several things, including the width of the stream the angler was intending to fish and the length of his rod. Walton preferred a line half the length of his rod. Cotton also hits upon the importance of the correct length of the flyline, saying that the length of the line is a mighty advantage to fishing at a distance. As Cotton writes, "To fish fine and far off is the first and principle rule of trout angling."

# Braiding A Flyline

I have found that braiding several horse hairs together to create a flyline is a sound method. Braiding, while it may look complex, is actually quite easy. There are only a few steps that are then repeated until the braid is finished.

First, wash the hairs in warm water and mild soap and let them dry. Wax them well with tying wax. Waxing the hairs will keep them soft and make them easy to work with.

Knot three hairs together at one end and secure this knot on a nail or ask your gillie to hold it steady as you begin to braid.

Hold the right hair between the thumb and forefinger of your right hand; the middle hair in your right hand between your forefinger and your middle finger; and the left hair between the thumb and forefinger of your left hand.

Bring the right hair over the middle hair placing the right hair in the middle. You'll now be holding that hair in between the forefinger and middle finger of your left hand.

Next, bring the left hair over the middle hair. This hair will now be held between the forefinger and the middle fingers of your right hand. Be sure to keep an equal tension on all three hairs.

Repeat the process until all the materials are used up.

Upon completion of the braid, secure the end of the braid with an overhand knot.

Follow the steps on the next pages to connect the links and finish the flyline.

*Note: To better illustrate braiding techniques, I used twine. To braid a true flyline, I would use horse hair.*

*The Colonial Angler's Manual of Flyfishing and Flytying*

Upon completion of all your links the next step is to knot the links together. The preferred knot is the water knot. Tie two over-hand knots, each around the standing end of the link.

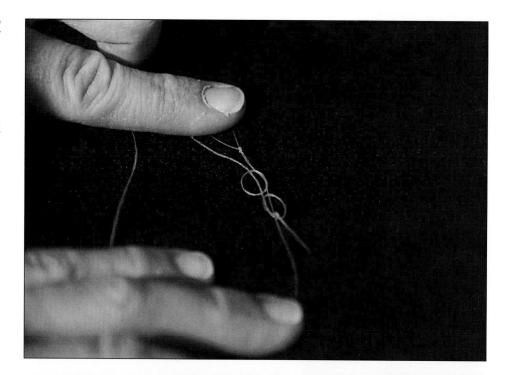

After all the links are knotted together you must now wrap each knot with silk. This will tie in the loose ends and cover the knot so nothing will catch on the line.

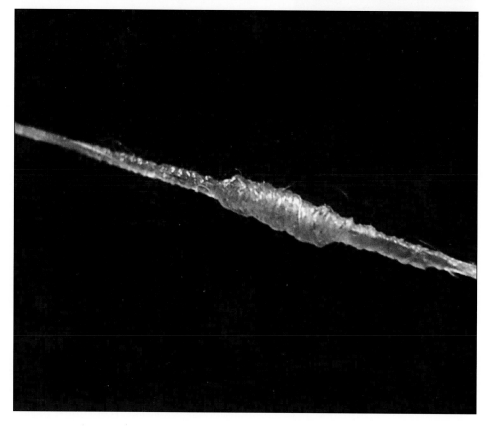

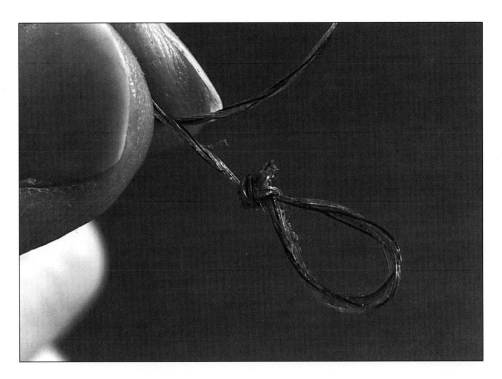

Make a loop on each end of the line and tie it with a fisherman's knot. Note that this photo shows a dark hair braided into this particular link. The dark hair will help to camouflage the line. This is the only time the use of the weaker dark hairs is permitted.

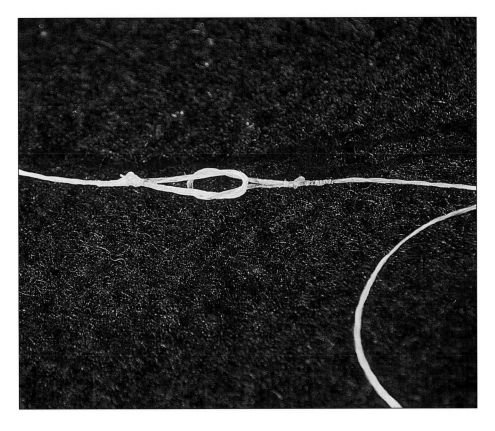

The fastest and easiest way to change a braided line is with a loop-to-loop connection.

The croppe section of the rod shows the proper use of horse tail. Here, you can see the line as it runs from the tip of the rod to the fly. To connect the line to the tip of the rod, lay a small section of the flyline against the tip. Wrap red tying silk around the tip and the line to bind the two together. The loop-to-loop connection was used to attach the fly to the flyline.

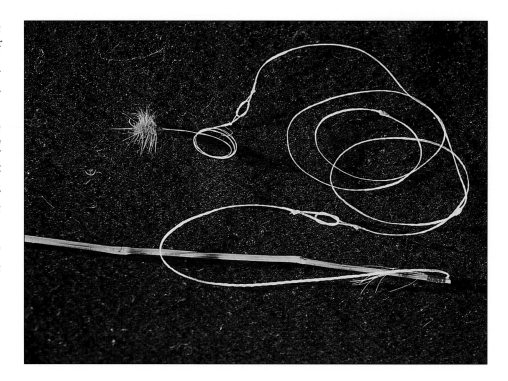

# Chapter Seven
# The Bended Hook

*Then let your Hooke be sure and strongly placed unto your lowest Linke with Silke or Hayre…*

John Dennys

*The Colonial Angler makes his own hooks for his angling needs.*

In this modern generation of angling, we have the finest flytying hooks available to us. Hook manufacturers are constantly producing new styles and bends to accommodate our tying demands. In fact, one could say we are quite spoiled. We often get upset and down right cranky when we can't find a flytying hook to meet our requirements for a certain fly pattern. Hooks that are defective are also a great source of annoyance, especially if they have been just purchased. The presence of defective hooks is understandable, though. After all, the hook manufacturer produces thousands of hooks a year; a few defective hooks might slip through quality control sometimes. But the manufacturer usually adds one or two hooks to the hundred count for just that instance.

In spite of all of this finery, let us not forget the humble beginnings of hook making. The colonial angler made all of his hooks himself. Each hook was made by hand. The utmost care was taken while fashioning the hooks, for without this very important tool, the angler could not practice the fine art of flytying.

Because making hooks by hand was a time-consuming process, the colonial angler had to gauge his materials carefully before he began. Strong, straight needles or pieces of wire were commonly used for hook making. The better the materials the colonial angler started with, the better his hooks would be, and the less he'd have to repeat his hook making process.

My research into the actual making of hooks started with Dame Juliana Berners' *Treatyse*. She begins by listing the proper tools for hook making. First is a set of sharp files of different sizes; two pairs of pincers (blacksmith tongs), one large and one small; a small hammer; an anvil; hook benders; and a heat source—in this case, a charcoal fire. Hooks are made from sewing needles. Heavier needles, such as those used by tailors and shoemakers, were used for stronger hooks.

Also in the 18th century, coils of wire were used to make hooks. I have successfully used piano wire to make recreations of the colonial angler's hooks. The wire comes in 36-inch lengths and is available in many different gauges. Again, heavier gauge wire was used to make stronger hooks for catching larger fish. Because wire was not pointed on one end like a needle, the angler needed to perform the extra step of sharpening the end of a wire hook. This step was usually done before the hook had been bent.

Dame Juliana devotes part of her discourse on hook making to adding barbs to the hook. Following in the tradition of the colonial angler, I do not add barbs to my hooks. The colonial angler, because he was fishing for recreation and not for survival, often made a practice of releasing the fish after the catch. This allowed the fish to swim free and provide sport for another day.

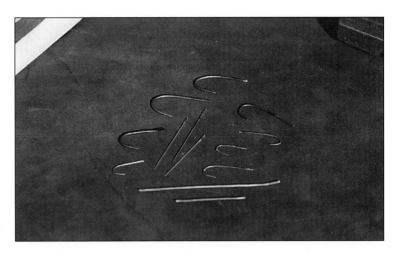

*The colonial angler needs to have a variety of hooks on hand; different fish require different hooks. Hooks for larger fish are made from stronger needles.*

Most likely, though, there may have been angler's during the colonial time period who followed Dame Juliana's *Treatyse* to the letter and created hooks with barbs. According to Dame Juliana, a barb would be lifted in the following manner after the needle has been annealed. Place a metal chisel a short distance from the end of the needle, about $5/16$". Hold the chisel at a slight angle on the needle and with a small hammer, strike the chisel smartly. Be careful not to hit the chisel too hard. A hard strike will cut the point off the needle. If performed correctly, striking the chisel will lift a

*The hook maker needs sharp files, pincers, a hammer, an anvil, and hook benders. With these tools, he can make hooks of every size and shape.*

*The Colonial Angler's Manual of Flyfishing and Flytying*

*Hook benders are basically forms around which a needle is bent to give it a desired shape. The hook bender on the left is made of hard wood with nails driven into the wood to shape the hook. The hook bender on the right is made entirely of wood. The nail keeps the needle in place as the hook is being bent.*

small piece of metal away from the needle or wire, creating a barb.

All hooks, whether they had a barb or not, were annealed before they were bent into shape. Annealing softens the metal, making it pliable so that it can be easily shaped into a hook.

To anneal the metal, Dame Juliana suggests securing the needle or length of wire in long-handled tongs and holding it in the flames of a charcoal fire. As the metal gets hotter, its color will change. Each color has its own temperature. When the metal glows a bright reddish-orange like the setting sun, it can be removed from the flame. The angler is now ready to bend the metal into the desired shape and size of hook to meet his particular tying needs.

When the metal was cool to the touch, the angler placed the tip of the needle or length of wire in a hook bender. Hook benders were simple devices made from wood. A carved, raised curve served as a form around which the metal could be bent. Another type of hook bender used nails pounded into the wood as a form for shaping the hook. Hook benders assured that all hooks conformed to the same basic curve.

Holding the opposite end of the metal in his hand, the angler used a downward pressure to bend the metal around the hook bender. If the shape he ended up with wasn't quite right, he could straighten the hook and rebend the metal. He must take care not to do this too often, though. Repeated bending of the metal may weaken it, causing the resulting hook to be weak.

Next, the angler cuts the shank of the hook to the desired length. The first tying hooks were of a very short shank length. The angler based the length of the shank on the insect he was trying to duplicate. Some of the smaller insects take a shorter shanked hook while larger insects take a longer shank.

The colonial angler usually made the shank of the hook one to three times greater than the gap of the hook. For example, if the gap between the bent end of the hook and the parallel shank measures one quarter of an inch, the shank should then measure one half of an inch to one inch. I've found that this is a good rule to follow, and I employ it in my hook making.

To cut the shank to size, the angler would lay the hook on a length of hard wood, place a chisel against the metal where he would like to cut it, and strike the chisel smartly with a small hammer. This will cut the hook to the proper size.

Once the hook is cut to size, the angler's next step is to hammer in the flat of the hook. He lays the hook on the anvil and, holding the hook in place with tongs, flattens the cut end of the hook with a hammer. Note that hooks of this time period did not have eyes, or holes, in the end through which the leader was attached.

Using a file, the angler then filed off any burrs that occurred on the flat part of the hook. This is an important step, for any sharp edges on this part of the hook may cause his flyline to tear.

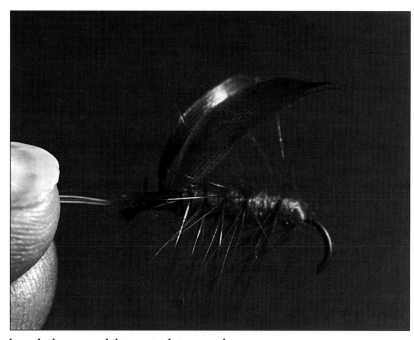

The angler's next step is to harden the hook. Holding the hook with blacksmith's tongs, he places the hook into the charcoal fire. Again, when the hook glows like the setting sun, he immediately immersed the red hot hook into water to cool. This process hardened the hook.

The next step, polishing the hook, was usually reserved for the angler's gillie. Using a file, he rubbed the scale off the hook until it was bright and shiny. This practice, according to Dame Juliana, keeps his hands busy and his mind in good thought.

When this process was complete, the angler had to draw the temper on the hooks. To do this, he placed the polished hook in the tongs and again holds the hook near the charcoal fire, heating the hook slowly. As the metal of the hook heated up, it changed color. The first color would be a light straw color, then a darker straw color. Then, the metal became a light bluish color, and finally the blue color darkened. When the hook reached the desired blue color, the angler immersed the hot hook into hot

*Rushing the hook-making process can result in a weak hook. This hook broke because the heating and bending were done too quickly.*

candle tallow to hold the deep blue color of the hook.

The angler's final step was to test the temper of the hook. To do this, the angler would stick the sharpened point of the finished hook into a piece of wood and bend it to test its strength. If the hook sprang back to shape, it was a good hook. If it broke, something went wrong with one of the heating processes and the hook was too brittle to use.

While hook making is a very time-consuming process, it is also very rewarding. Catching a fish on a hook that one has made by his own hand is indeed very rewarding.

Of course, not every angler has time to make his own hooks. For example, Izaak Walton does not give any direction on hook making in *The Compleat Angler,* but instead suggests that one seek out the best hook maker one can afford. His recommendation was Charles Kirby, who lived at Harp Alley on Shoe Lane, the best hook maker in London during Walton's time.

# Bending A Hook

Place the annealed needle (or piece of wire, if that is what you are using) in the hook bender. To bend the metal, the needle needs to be inserted between the nail and the raised form.

Before you begin to bend the metal, be sure that the needle is positioned correctly in the hook bender. Notice how far the point of the needle extends beyond the nail. This is necessary to achieve the correct length of the hook. Apply firm, even pressure on the needle as you bend it around the hook bender.

*The Colonial Angler's Manual of Flyfishing and Flytying*

Remove the bent hook from the hook bender. If you are not pleased with the shape of the hook, straighten the needle and begin again. Cut the shank of the hook to the correct length with a chisel.

Usually a length one to three times greater than the gap of the hook is preferred.

After the shanks are cut, the next step is to hammer the "flat" of the hook. Remember, the colonial angler's hook did not have an eye. Flattening the end of the hook will keep the flytying materials from slipping off the hook. File the flat smooth. Rough edges may cut the leader or arming thread.

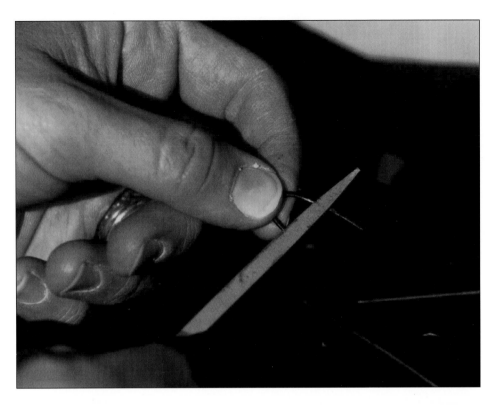

Harden the hook by heating the metal in a charcoal fire once again. When the metal glows red, remove the hook from the flame and immediately immerse it in cold water. Polish the hook with a file. Draw the temper on the hook to the color desired. Finally, sharpen the hook.

An optional step is to raise a barb on the hook. This step is usually done before bending the hook. Using a chisel and a hammer, place the chisel on the needle and strike the chisel smartly. This will lift a small piece of metal, forming a barb. Note: The use of a barbed hook by a colonial angler is quite controversial. The colonial angler, being a gentleman angler, practiced the catch-and-release method of angling.

# Chapter Eight
# The Properly Dressed Fly

*And now good master, proceed to your promised direction for making and ordering my artificial fly.*

In this modern age of flyfishing, with its infinite number of flytying tools and materials and all the new publications on tying techniques, is there really a need for one more set of flytying instructions? The answer is yes, especially if one is interested in the colonial angler's methods of flytying.

My research into the properly dressed fly became quite intensive. Not only were the materials used by the colonial angler different, he also had a different set of tools. Remember, anglers in the 18th century had no flytying vices, hackle pliers, whip finishers or bobbins, just to name a few of the conveniences we modern flytyers take for granted.

Because I chose to emulate the lifestyle, tools, equipment, and techniques of the colonial angler's time period, I had to research my subject thoroughly in order to recreate it correctly. Only with accurate information could I put all I learned to the ultimate test of truly recreating the flies used by the colonial angler.

A good introduction to this chapter comes from 18th-century writer John Gay. The following quote is taken from his book, *Rural Sports*, written in 1720.

*Around the steal no tortured worm shall tweine*
*No blood of living insect stain my line:*
*Let me, less cruel, cast he feathered hook,*
*With pliant rod across the pebbled brook.*

Gay's writing also provided me with information on how to look to the living insects as models for creating artificial patterns.

*To frame the little animal, provide*
*All the gay hues that wait on female pride;*
*Let nature guide thee. Sometimes golden wire*
*The shining bellies of the fly require;*
*The peacock's plumes the tackle must not fail,*
*Nor the deer purchase of the sable's tail.*
*Each gaudy bird some slender tribute brings,*
*And lends the growin insects proper wings:*
*Silks of all colors must their aid impart,*
*End every fur promote the fisher's art.*

As the angler sat along the banks of his favorite streams, he contemplated the living insects and how to best duplicate them. Possibly this is what our forefathers did as they watched the insects upon the water. They may have asked themselves how to imitate the fly on a hook using the proper materials of their time.

The colonial anglers also studied the insects as they moved upon the water. They noticed how the trout fed upon the insects as they swam downstream. Undoubtedly this is why the mentors of the colonial angler gave directions on how to angle with an artificial offering.

*It is stated that the colonial angler's dubbing bag should include everything in the world.*

## The Colonial Angler's Flytying Materials

It is stated that the dubbing bag should contain everything in the world.... For the colonial angler, nothing could be more correct. In his dubbing bag, he carried all the materials he needed to tie his flies, repair a broken flyline, or add another hook. Sometimes, after watching to see what insects the fish were interested in, he would even tied a fly while sitting on the bank of the stream.

In my dubbing bag, I also carry everything in the world—or at least everything that is available to me in this, the 20th century. Some of the common materials the colonial angler used, such as the fur or feathers of a now endangered species, are not available today. Nor should they be. If you are planning to emulate the colonial angler, as I did, be sure not to use the furs or feathers of any endangered species. We are still gentlemen anglers, with a deep regard for nature and the law, and do not want to create a demand for exotic feathers and furs.

If a certain material was not available to me, either because the species was endangered or the material was not readily available, I researched different materials until I found a suitable replacement. For example, I have had to substitute other materials for hawk feathers, monkey fur, seal fur, owl feathers and heron feathers, just to name a few.

Looking backward through our angling heritage it is interesting to find out what materials the colonial angler used and how these materials were obtained. Simplicity was the key to a successful pattern. Just like today, if the colonial angler did not have the correct color of a given material, he dyed the material he had to suit his needs.

This enclosed list of materials was garnered from the dubbing bag of Richard Bowlker, who wrote *The Art of Angling* in 1746.

*The fur of seals, moles, and water-rats; black, blue, purple, white and violet goat's hair, commonly called mohair; camlets of every color; furs from the necks and ears of hares; also hackle feathers from the neck and ears of cocks, red dun, yellowish, white and black.*

*For the wings of flies, feathers from the neck, breast, and wings of the wild mallard, partridge and pheasant; also the wings of the blackbird, brown hen, starling, jay, land rail, swallow, thrush, field fare, and a water coot; with peacock's and ostrich's plumes.*

*Provide also marking-silk of all colors; gold and silver plated wire or twist a sharp knife, hooks of every size, a needle, and a pair of sharp pointed scissors.*

The dubbing (the body of the fly) should never, when it is possible to avoid it, be made of wool, which becomes heavy when wet, but of mohair which resists the water and preserves its color.

*A rich dun dubbing may be procured by combing, with a fine toothed comb, the back of a lead colored greyhound. Hog's fur which grows between the roots of the bristles, dyed of various colors, bear's fur, fox's fur, fur off the belly of a hedge hog, the light yellow fur from the martin's neck, are all useful as dubbing. Dubbing of various hues and of excellent quality, resisting the water well and not losing their color when in it, are to be found in tan years among the hairs that fall off the skins, and likewise among pieces of plaster that are stripped from old walls or ceilings. Lime not only changes the original color of hair, but adds to its capability of withstanding water. The brighter and finer the gold and silver twist used in ribbing flies, the better.*

Bowlker also mentions quite a few other materials and tips for tying flies. According to Bowlker, the scarcest and best hackles were duns of all shades, particularly those which have the clearest different shades of blue; furnace hackles of a red color with a black streak along the stem up the middle of the feather; red hackles, light and dark ginger; black and grizzled hackles. He suggests that hackles should be taken from the upper part of the necks of full-grown cocks. Here, the hackles grow from half an inch to two inches long.

When dun hackles cannot be procured from cocks, Bowlker instructs the angler to use those from dun hens; but they are, from the softness of their fiber, less capable of resisting water as well as those of a male bird. The best time for plucking birds, according to Bowlker, is in the middle of winter. (Note that plucking a feather was a common practice for this did not kill the rooster from which the angler got a good hackle. A properly cared for rooster will live 10 to 12 years and give the angler plenty of tying material. Warm olive oil was always rubbed on the bird's resulting bald spot to protect it from infection.)

*With the proper flytying materials set before him, The Colonial Angler ties an artificial fly for use on the stream that day. Anglers would often tie flies to "match the hatch" if that particular fly was not included with their array of flies. Sometimes these flies were tied streamside, just as The Colonial Angler does here.*

Bowlker mentions that excellent hackles may be taken from the back of the grouse, the tail of the common wren, the breast and back of the partridge, the outside part, nearest the body, of the golden plover's wing, and the inside of the snipe's wing.

To be brief, the fly-maker will seize upon everything that may be of any possibility of use.

## Cotton's Green Drake

For a good example of the proper materials and the correct colors, let's look to Cotton's description of the Green Drake. By the standards of the time (1676) this was a very complex fly to tie. Despite its complexity, it is a very popular pattern and still in use today.

For the fun of it, let's look to find the proper material for this pattern. Note that we will be using only the materials given. I will not substitute in any modern materials, for all the materials of the 18th century are available today.

### Hook

The Green Drake is tied upon a large hook. Observe the natural insect to see how long the shank of the hook should be as no size was given in the original pattern.

### Body material

A: Camel's hair. Natural, not dyed.

*Cotton's Green Drake per his tying instructions circa 1676.*

B: Bright bear's hair. The under fur.

C: The soft down that is combed from a hog's bristles, better known as pig's wool. (Note: This is a fun material to collect. Some books mention how to obtain this material. The body material was the short, fine hair on a pig's face. To secure the material, the person was required to shave the pig's face. Another mention of how to get pig's wool instructs the angler to take it from the underside of the pig's belly. The fur on the underside of the pig is soft and pinkish, a very desirable flytying material used in this time period. This material dubbs fairly well and makes a good translucent body which retains its luster and color when wet.)

D: Camlet. Made from camel hair and mixed with wool, silk, and cotton to form a material or cloth fabric, then dyed to the proper color. In this case a yellow camlet was used. This material is used quite often in the older flytying patterns.

E: Green silk or yellow silk, waxed with green wax. This green-colored silk is used for the body. The body is long, meaning that the natural insect is larger than most, and ribbed about with the silk. (Silks of every color and size are a must. To aid in the correct body color, wax was often used as mentioned here. Many of the flytying instructions suggest the use of a colored wax for a given fly pattern.

*The evolution of the Palmer-style fly. Modern anglers simply add red wool for a tail and they now have the ever popular Woolly Worm.*

### Tail material

The wisps of the tail hair are made from the long hairs of sables. The sable is a weasel-like mammal of northern Europe. It has glossy, dark fur, black in color. The hair from fitchets, European pole cats with tail hairs similar to a sables', may be used.

*Wing material*

Wings. Made of a white-grey mallard feather dyed yellow. The use of duck wings have been used throughout the centuries for proper wing material. Cotton used the shaved root of a barbary tree to achieve the correct yellow color for this fly. He boiled the feathers, along with the shavings and "as much alum as a walnut," in rain water. For most of us it is probably best for to use modern dyes to gain the proper colors.

## The Hackled Fly and the Palmer-style Fly

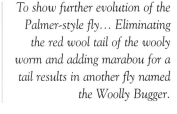

*To show further evolution of the Palmer-style fly... Eliminating the red wool tail of the wooly worm and adding marabou for a tail results in another fly named the Woolly Bugger.*

T he term hackle refers to a feather from the neck-hackle or the saddle-hackle of a rooster, partridge, or grouse. These feathers are used to create the legs of an artificial fly. One fly pattern consists of only a body with hackles wound spindly about its body. This particular style of fly pattern is known as the Palmer. It resembles the bristling, fuzzy appearance of a caterpillar.

The hackled fly refers to a fly on which the hackles are would about the head three or four times. Our first artificial fly, the Red Hackle, derives its name from the cock red hackle feathers. The body dressing further identifies it. The hackles, or Palmers, are made with various colored bodies, such as black, green, red and yellow or peacock, with either black, red, brown or gray legs.

*For the final step of the evolution of the Palmer-style fly... Here, the tail was simply eliminated. Now add elk hair fur and over wing and you have the Elk Hair Caddis, a very popular fly pattern of this modern generation. When one adds a new material, a new fly pattern is created. Nothing new, just a new application of flytying materials to an old basic pattern.*

*The Colonial Angler's Manual of Flyfishing and Flytying*

# Tying a Red Hackle

The fly I am tying in this series of pictures is a Red Hackle. Before I start to tie the actual fly, I need to arm the hook with leader material. Hold the hook between the forefinger and thumb of your left hand. The tying vices that are used by modern flyfishermen had not yet been invented. This is truly a hand-tied fly.

With a scissors, cut approximately one yard of silk thread. The color of the silk thread should match the body color of the fly you are tying. For a Red Hackle, use white silk thread. Wax the silk well, drawing the silk between your fingers and thumb. This helps to waterproof the tying silk and helps the tying materials to stay in place and hold more securely on the hook.

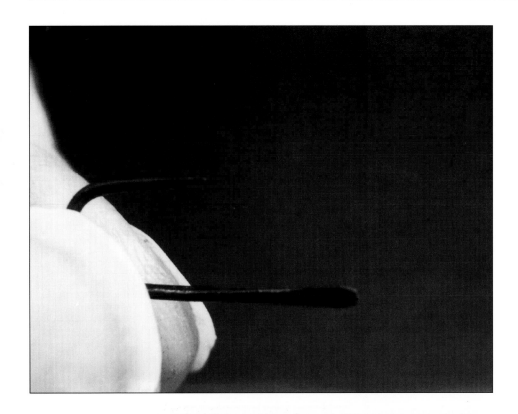

Place the hook in your left hand, between the thumb and forefinger, hold the hook so that the point is up. The hook is held in this fashion so as to prevent you from being stuck by the hook while you are tying the fly.

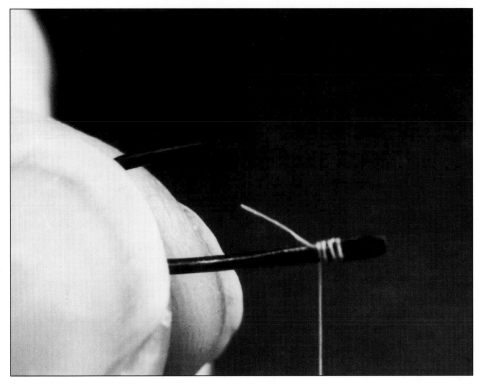

Take the waxed silk thread in your right hand and wrap the entire length of the shank of the hook. Wrap the shank of the hook to the bend and then forward to the flat of the hook. Please remember that 18th-century hooks did not have eyes. To keep the silk secure, finish off with a simple half-hitch. Do not cut the tying silk. It is important to wrap the entire shank so the horse-tail leader has a bed of silk upon which to lie.

In this picture I am separating the horse tail for the leader. Please note that the hairs must be all the same diameter and free from scars. I usually use three hairs next the hook. The hairs should be at least 12″ to 18″ in length.

Hold the hook between the thumb and forefinger of your left hand. Place the three hairs on the inside of the hook so that they extend past the bend of the hook about 2–3″. Pinch the hairs against the hook with the thumb and forefinger of your left hand. With your right hand, wrap the silk about the hook to tie in your horse-tail leader. When the horse tail is securely tied in, use a half-hitch to secure the tying silk so it will not unwind.

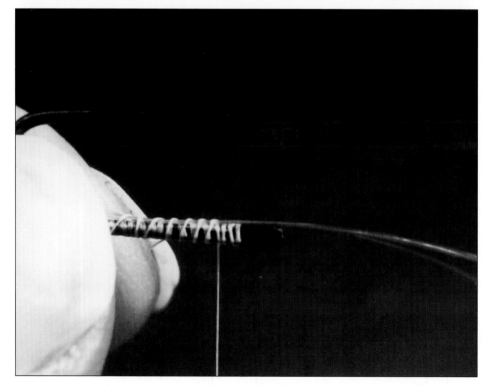

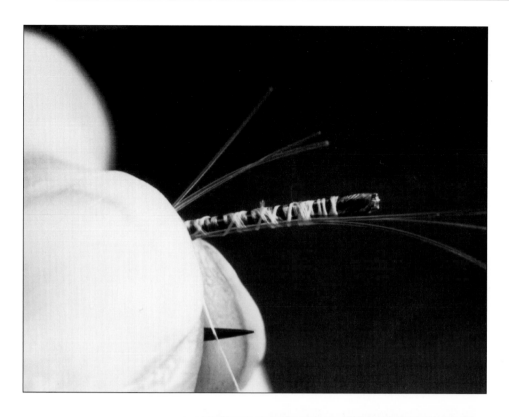

Turn the hook around so
the hook shank is up. Fold
the 2–3" of extra horse
hair toward the front of
the hook. Tie in the hairs
the full length of the shank
by wrapping the silk to the
bend of the hook. Tie off
the tying silk with a half-
hitch. Keep the silk thread
waxed to keep the knot
from coming undone. The
hook is now armed with a
horse-tail leader and is
ready to accept any fly
dressing you may wish to
tie.

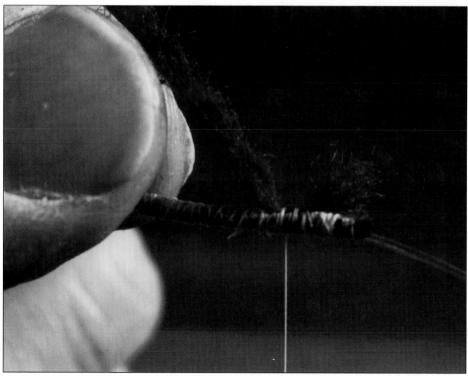

Tie in the body of red
wool yarn. Hold the hook
so the point is up. Lay the
yarn on the shank of the
hook with one end of the
wool even with the end of
the shank. Allow the
excess to lie between the
thumb and forefinger of
your left hand. With your
right hand, wrap the
waxed tying silk about the
hook securing the wool to
the body. Bring the tying
silk forward to the flat of
the hook, and secure your
silk with a half-hitch.

Wrap the wool yarn from the bend of the hook forward to the flat of the hook. Secure the yarn body with 2 half-hitches. Leave room so you can hackle the fly. Do not crowd the body material too close to the flat of the hook.

Take two cock red hackles that grew under a cock's wattles. Remove any excess fluff from the hackle and fasten the hackles to the hook. Secure the stems of the hackles with the waxed tying silk. Tie off the silk with a half-hitch.

While holding the hook in your left hand, wrap the hackles about the hook, with your right hand. First wrap one hackle and secure with tying silk. Next, wrap the second hackle in the same way. (Do not rely on the modern convenience of a hackle pliers to complete this step.)

Wrap a nice head with your tying silk, and secure the tying silk with three half-hitches. Trim off any excess tying silk.

The next step is to braid the leader onto the fly. Follow the braiding instructions on page 51. Be sure to keep the braid nice and tight and the horse tail waxed. When the leader is braided secure the ends of the horsetail with an overhand knot. This will keep the braid from unwinding. Keep the leader waxed so it will be easier to handle.

There are many various kinds of loop knots. A proper knot, and my personal preference, is the fisherman's loop. This is one of the strongest knots you can use to tie a loop in the end of the leader. (Note: The fisherman's loop is commonly known in this modern generation as the perfection loop.)

When the knot for the loop is made, wrap the knot with silk thread. Cover the entire knot with silk. Again, be sure to keep the thread waxed. Secure the silk thread with a half-hitch. Trim off any excess silk.

The finished red hackle, with three hairs next to the hook. Also shown is the finished braided loop.

# Tying the Palmer-Worm

Hold the hook in your left hand. Follow the steps on pages 72–75 to arm the hook with the horse-tail leader. When the hook is armed with leader, select two hackle feathers from a cock red or capon's neck. Remove the fluff from the stem. Hold the hackles at the bend of the hook with your left hand. With your right hand, tie in the stems of the hackles with the tying silk. Secure the silk with a half-hitch.

Next install the body. Use the same techniques for wrapping the body of the red hackle on pages 75–76. I am using substitute red seal fur. I believe that when I dress the old-style fly patterns, I should use the materials per the descriptions given. But, I will not use any fur or feather from a protected or endangered species.

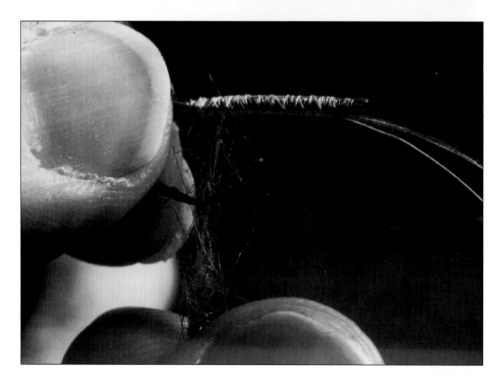

Wrap the dubbed silk about the hook, forward to the head of the fly and secure the dubbing with a half-hitch.

While still holding the hook in your left hand, wind the hackles with the right hand forward to the head of the fly in a spiraling fashion (called the Palmer method) about the hook. The hackles can be wound one at a time or both hackles together.

*The Colonial Angler's Manual of Flyfishing and Flytying*

When the hackles are wound about the hook, hold them in place with a free finger of your left hand. Tie in the hackles with the tying silk. Remove the excess hackle tips with a scissors. Make a nice head on the fly with the tying silk and finish with three half-hitches. Keep the silk waxed, and trim off the silk.

To complete the fly, braid the leader and add the loop described in the red hackle fly on pages 78–79.

# Tying a Soldier Palmer

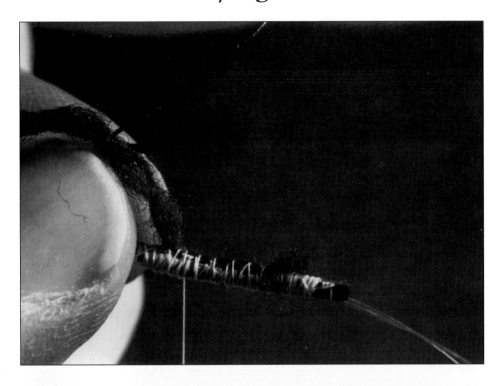

Arm the hook following the steps on 72–75. When the hook is armed, tie in a 6″ length of gold thread at the bend of the hook. Select two hackle feathers from a cock red or capon's neck. Remove the fluff from the stem. Holding the hackle feathers next to the hook, tie in the stems of the hackles with tying silk. Secure the silk at the bend of the hook with a half-hitch. Tie in the red wool for the body. Wrap the tying silk forward; secure with a half-hitch.

The hook is still held with the left hand. The right hand is used to wrap the body material forward about the hook. Palmer the hackles forward, then wrap the gold thread forward through the hackles. Be careful not to tie down any barbules of the hackle. If you do, pick them out with a needle.

When all body materials and hackles are tied in, wrap a nice head with the tying silk. Secure with half-hitches and trim off any excess tying silk.

When the fly is completed, follow the steps on pages 78–79 to braid the leader and add the loop.

# Tying the May Fly

Now, let's look to Izaak Walton for his instructions on how to tie a fly. As you'll remember, Walton's book *The Compleat Angler* is written as a discourse between the instructor, Piscator, and the pupil, Venator. Here, Walton is discussing the proper method of tying flies with his pupil Venator. The directions that follow are also quoted from Walton's book. The photographs that accompany the steps are of me demonstrating Walton's instructions.

> *I shall next give you some other directions for fly-fishing, such as are given by Mr. Thomas Barker, a gentlemen that had spent much time in fishing; but I shall do it with a variation. [Note, Barker wrote* The Art of Angling *in 1651.]*
>
> *In the middle of March, till which time, a man should not honesty, catch a trout— or in April, if the weather be dark, or a little windy or cloudy, the best fishing is with the palmer-worm, of which I last spoke to you; but of these there diverse kinds, or at least of diverse color; these and the May-fly are the ground of all fly-angling, which are to be thus made:*

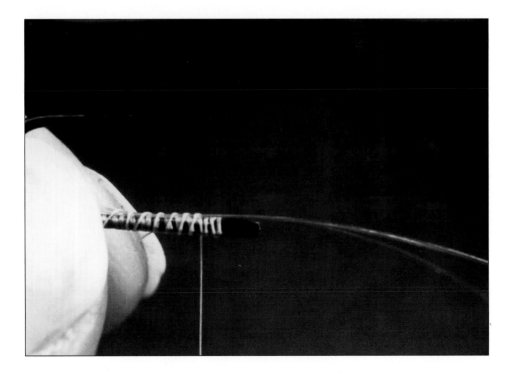

*First, you must arm your hook with this line in the inside of it.*

Then take your scissors,
and cut so much of a
brown mallard's feather,
as in you own reason will
make of it.

Then lay the outmost part
of your feather next to
your hook, then the point
of your feather next the
shank of your hook;

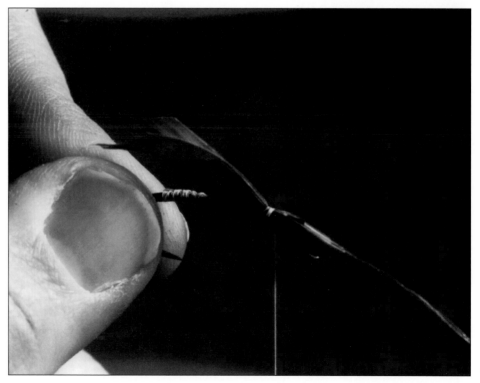

and having so done, whip it three or four times about the hook with the same silk with which your hook was armed.

And having made the silk fast, take the hackle of a cock or capon's neck, take off the one side of the feather, and then take the hackle,

silk, or crewel, gold or silver thread, (optional)
make fast at the bend of
the hook, that is to say,
below your arming.

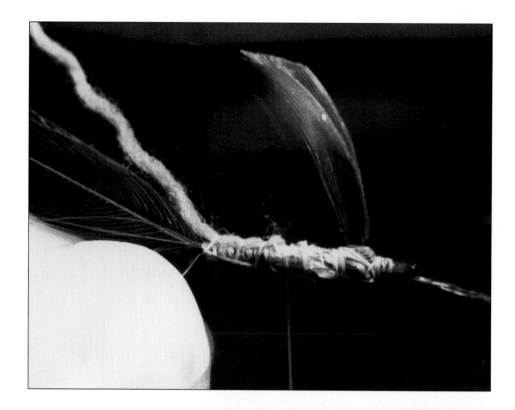

Then you must take the
silk, or crewel, gold, or silver thread, and work it up
to the wings, shift or still
removing your finger, as
you turn the silk about the
hook; and still looking at
every stop or turn, that
your gold, or what materials severe you make your
fly of do lie right and
neatly; and if you find
they do so, then, when
you have made the head,
make all fast;

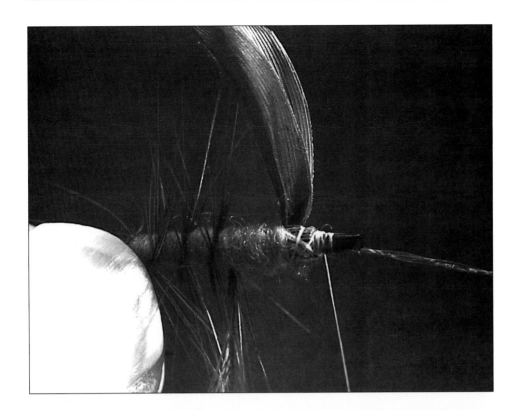

*and then work you hackle up to the head, and make that fast:*

*and then with a needle or pin divide the wing into two, and then with the arming silk whip it about crossways betwixt the wings, and then with your thumb you must turn the point of the feather towards the bend of the hook, and then work three or four times about the shank of the hook,…*

*and then view the proportion, and if all be neat and to your liking, fasten.*

Follow steps on pages 78-79 to braid the leader and add the loop. By Walton's description this is the completed May Fly.

*The Colonial Angler's Manual of Flyfishing and Flytying*

# Dame Juliana's List of Twelve Perfect Flies

This list of fly patterns from A *Treatyse of Fysshynge with an Angle* is attributed to Dame Juliana Berners. The popularity of these flies has held firm throughout many generations of flyfishermen.

Even Izaak Walton reveals in *The Compleat Angler* that Dame Juliana's flies are indeed the the perfect twelve wet flies. He was so pleased with these patterns, that it is said he did not change a single one.

**March Dun Fly**

*#1 March—The Dun Fly*. The body is made of dun wool; the wings from the partridge's feathers.

**March Dun Fly**

*#2 March—Another Dun Fly*. The body is made of black wool; the wings of the black drake's feathers and the feathers from under the jay's wing and tail.

#3 *April—The Stone Fly*. The body is made of black wool; made yellow under the wings and under the tail, and so made with the wings of the drake.

**April Stone Fly**

#4 *May—The Ruddy Fly*. The body is made of red wool wrapped about with black silk; the feathers are from the wings of the drake and the feathers of a red capon also, those that hang dangling on his sides next to his tail.

**May Ruddy Fly**

#5 May—*The Yellow Fly*. The body is made of yellow wool; and the wings of the red cock's hackle, and of the drake slightly yellow.

**May Yellow Fly**

#6 May—*The Black Looper*. The body is made of black wool, and lapped about with the head of a peacock's tail; the wings are made of the wings of a brown capon, with his blue feathers in his head.

**May Black Looper**

#7 *June—The Dun Cut.* The body is made of black wool, with a yellow list on either side; and the wings are from the wings of a buzzard, bound with black braided hemp.

**June Dun Cut**

#8 *June—The Moorish Fly.* Made with the body of darkish wool; the wings are made of the blackish mail of the drake.

**June Moorish Fly**

**June Tawny Fly**

*#9 June—The Tawny Fly.* The body is made of a tawny wool; the wings are made contrary one against the other from the whitish mail of the wild drake.

**July Wasp Fly**

*#10 July—The Wasp Fly.* The body is made of black wool, lapped about with yellow silk; the wings are made of the feathers of the drake or of the buzzard.

#11 July—The Shell Fly. The body is made of greenish wool, lapped about with the head of a peacock's tail and the wings of the buzzard.

**July Shell Fly**

#12 August—The Drake Fly. The body made with black wool, lapped about with black silk; the wings are made with the mail of the black drake, with a black head.

**August Drake Fly**

**The Fly Patterns of Charles Cotton**

For this last section on the properly dressed fly, I must include the fly patterns of Charles Cotton (1676). This is the next series of flies listed in the long line of the evolution of the historical documentation of fly patterns.

### January

Cotton suggests using a **Red Brown** and a **Dun Gnat**. The Red Brown has a brown body and white wings. The wings are made from the almost white mails of a mallard. The body is made from the tail of a black cur. Cotton cautions that the hair of a smooth-coated dog of the same color won't do because it will not dye well, but retain its natural color. The dun gnat is a very bright, little fly. It is to be made as small as it possibly can be. The body is made from a mixed dubbing of martin's fur and the white of a hare's scut (a scut is a short, stumpy tail). The wings are also white and very small.

A note on the hook sizes of the fly patterns: Cotton does not list hook sizes. In order to tie one of Cotton's flies properly, one must observe the natural insect to duplicate the insect's size.

### February

This month Cotton suggests a **Lesser Red Brown**, similar to the red brown used last month. The dubbing of this fly must be of a blacker color, wrapped with red silk. The dubbing for this fly should be from the black spot of a hog's ear. "Not that a black spot in any part of the hog will not afford the same color," Cotton says, "but that the hair in that place is, by many degrees, softer, and more fit of the purpose."

Also, this month, Cotton suggests a **Plain Hackle,** or Palmer-fly, made with a rough black body from black spaniel's fur or the whirl of an ostrich's feather and the red hackle of a capon. The **Lesser Hackle** and the **Great Hackle** can also be used with good results this month. The great hackle is best used upon whirling round water for hooking very great fish. One Great Hackle is of a black body, ribbed over with silver and a red feather over all. Another Great Hackle uses gold instead of silver.

Two dun flies can be used this month, according to Cotton. First is a **Great Dun.** The body is made with dun bear's hair, and the wings are made of the grey feather found near a mallard's tail. Second is the **Great Blue Dun.** Use the bottom of a bear's hair next to the roots mixed with a little blue camlet. The wings are made of a mallard's dark gray feathers.

Also this month, use a bark brown with dubbing of the brown hair off the flank a branded cow and wings of the gray drake's feather. Note that these

*The Colonial Angler's Manual of Flyfishing and Flytying*

several **Palmer Flies** are altered in size and color depending on the water and the sky. They can be used in this month and all other months of the year when you are not certain what fly to use.

*March*

For this month, Cotton suggests you are to use all the same hackles and flies as in the previous months, but you are to make them smaller.

We have also for this month, a little dun, called a **Whirling Dun.** The dubbing is made from the bottom fur of a squirrel's tail, and the wing is made from the gray feather of a drake.

Also use a **Bright Brown** with dubbing either of the brown of a spaniel, or that of a red cow's flank, and gray wings. A **Whitish Dun** should be made from the roots of camel's hair with wings of a mallard's gray feathers.

Another fly for this month is the **Thorn-tree Fly.** Its dubbing is black, mixed with eight or ten hairs of a kind of "Isabella-colored" mohair. This unusual name for the color of the mohair comes from a Spanish tale that Cotton retells. "The Archduke Albertus, who had married the Infanta Isabella, daughter of Philip II, of Spain, with whom he had the low countries in dowry, in the year 1602. Having determined to lay siege to Ostend, then in the possession of the heretics, his pious princess who attended him in that expedition, made a vow, that until it was taken, she would not change her clothes. Contrary to expectation, as the story says, it was three years before the archduke succeeded, in which her highness's linen had acquired the above mentioned hue." The body of the fly should be made as little as can be made and of a bright mallard's feather.

Another **Blue Dun** is made from the hairs of a black-gray hound. Cotton instructs the angler to take a small-tooth comb and comb the hound's neck. He says the down that sticks in the teeth of the comb will be the finest blue the angler ever saw. The wings of this fly cannot be too white. Use this fly from the tenth of the month until the 24th.

Also use a **Little Black Gnat,** the dubbing of which is made from the fur of a black water-dog or the down of a young coot ,and the wings of which are made from the white mail of a mallard. The body should be as little as you can possibly make it, and the wings should be as short as the body.

From the sixteenth of this month, use a **Bright Brown.** The dubbing of this fly should be made from the hair of an abortive calf dipped in a skinner's lime-pits. The lime will turn the hair so bright that it will shine like gold. Cotton suggests using the feather of a brown hen for the wings. This fly can be used until the tenth of April.

*April*

Take all the same hackles and flies that were taken in March. Cotton suggests changing the browns so that they are lapped with red silk. The duns should also be changed so that they are lapped with yellow.

To these flies, add a **Small Bright Brown,** made of spaniel's fur with a light gray wing. Also take a **Little Dark Brown,** the dubbing should be made of dark brown mixed with violet camlet. The wings are made from a mallard's gray feather.

From the twelfth of this month, Cotton suggests using a **Whirling Dun,** commonly made of the ash-colored down of a fox cub, ribbed with yellow silk. The wings are made from the pale gray feather of a mallard.

There is also a **Yellow Dun,** with the dubbing of camel's hair mixed with yellow camlet or wool and a white-gray wing. Also take another **Little Brown,** with a dubbing of a dark brown and violet camlet and a gray wing.

From the twentieth of this month use what Cotton calls a **Horse-flesh Fly,** the dubbing of which is a blue mohair mixed with with pink and red wool, a light colored wing, and a dark brown head.

Many times Cotton's descriptions include the word stuff. What does stuff refer to? Ask any seamstress and she will tell you that stuff is the beginnings of making woolen material and what is left over. This stuff makes great body material.

*May*

During this month, Cotton suggests angling with a **Turkey Fly,** the dubbing raveled out of some blue stuff and lapped about with yellow silk; the wings, of a mallard's gray feather.

Also take a **Great Hackle** or a palmer fly with a yellow body, ribbed with gold-twist. The large wings are made from a mallard's feather dyed yellow. A red capon's hackle is added over all.

Then take a **Black Fly,** with the dubbing of a black spaniel fur; and the wings of a mallard's gray feather.

After that, take a **Light Brown** with a slender body. The dubbing for this fly should be twirled upon small red silk and raised with the point of a needle so that the ribs of brown of silk may show through. The wings are made of a mallard's gray feather

Next, use a **Little Dun** with the dubbing of a bear's dun whirled upon yellow silk. The wings are to be made of the gray feather of a mallard.

Then, take a simple **White Gnat** with a pale wing and a black head.

Cotton also suggests for this month a fly called the **Peacock Fly.** The body is made from the whirl of a peacock's feather with a red head. The wings are made from a mallard's feather.

Next is the **Dun Cut,** the dubbing of which is a bear's dun, with a little blue and yellow mixed with in. Add a large dun wing and two horns at the head made from the hairs of a squirrel's tail.

The next fly is called a **Cow-Lady.** It is a little fly made from the body, of a peacock's feather. The wing is made from a red feather or from strips of the red hackle of a cock.

Then there is the **Cow-Dung Fly.** The dubbing of this fly is light brown mixed with yellow. The wing is the dark gray feather of a mallard.

The artificial **Green Drake,** is made upon a large hook. The dubbing is camel's hair, bright bear's hair, pig's wool, and yellow camlet mixed together. The body is long and ribbed about with green silk, or yellow silk waxed with green wax. The tail is from the long hairs of the sable of Fitchet, and the wings are the white-gray feather of a mallard dyed yellow. This fly is used from about the twentieth of this month until the beginning of June.

The **Gray Drake** is very similar to the green drake and should be taken also. Make the body from pig's wool and black spaniel's fur mixed well together and ribbed with black silk. The tail is made from the long hairs of a black cat's beard and the wing of the black grey feather of a mallard.

The **Stone Fly** can be used as early as the middle of April, but according to Cotton, it is never taken well until the middle of May. Its body is made with dear's dun, and brown and yellow camlet mixed together well. Make the dubbing more yellow on the belly near the tail when you dub the body. The tail is three hairs from a black cat's beard. The body is ribbed with yellow silk, and the wings are long and large and made from the dark gray feathers of a mallard. The Stone Fly can be used until almost the end of June.

The next is a may fly called the **Black Fly.** It has a black body, whirled with an ostrich-feather and ribbed with silver twist. The black hackle of a cock is wrapped over all. (This suggests this pattern is a palmer type).

The **Little Yellow May Fly** is exactly the same shape as the green drake, but smaller. It is made of a bright yellow camlet. The wings are made from a white-gray feather dyed yellow.

The last fly of this month is called the **Camlet Fly.** It is made of a dark brown shining camlet, ribbed with a very small light green silk. The wings are the double gray feathers of a mallard.

*June*

Cotton suggests taking the **Green Drake** and **Stone Fly.**

Late at night, from the 12th to the 24th, take a fly the **Owl Fly.** This fly is made from a weasel's tail with white-gray wings. Another dun, called the **Barn Fly** from its yeasty color, is made from the fur of a yellow dun cat and the gray feathers of a mallard.

Cotton also notes that a hackle with a purple body whipped about with a red capon's feather should be used this month. Also take a **Gold Twist Hackle** with a purple body whipped about with a red capon's feather. This pattern is similar to the above hackle, only with a gold twist ribbed throughout the body.

To these, Cotton adds a **Flesh Fly,** made from a back spaniel's fur mixed with blue wool and a gray wing. Another **Little Flesh Fly** is made from the whirl of a peacock's feather. The wings are made from the gray feather of drake. The body and wing of the **Peacock Fly** are both made of the feathers of a peacock.

There is also the flying ant, or the **Ant Fly,** with the dubbing of brown and red camlet mixed. The wings are a light gray.

We also have a **Brown Gnat** with a very slender body of brown and violet camlet well-mixed and a light gray wing. Another fly is the **Little Black Gnat** with the dubbing of black mohair and a white-gray wing.

Cotton also tells us to take a **Green Grasshopper.** The dubbing for this fly is of green and yellow wool mixed. It is ribbed over with green silk with a red capon's feather over all. Lastly, take a **Little Dun Grasshopper.** The body of this fly is slender and made of a dun camlet with a dun hackle at the top.

## July

First, Cotton suggest taking all the small flies that were taken in June along with the following flies.

The **Orange Fly** is made with a body of orange wool, and the wings are made from a black feather.

Also take a **Little Whitish Dun** with a body of white mohair and the wings of a blue heron's feather.

The **Wasp Fly** is made from the fur of a black cat's tail ribbed about with yellow silk. The wing is made from the gray feather of a mallard.

Another fly taken this month is a **Black Hackle.** The body is made from the whirl of a peacock's feather with black hackle feather on the top. A second Black Hackle body is made without wings from a peacock's whirl.

Also take the **Shell Fly.** The dubbing of this fly is yellow-green Jersey wool with a little white hog's hair mixed in.Cotton suggests that the best way to hit the right color is to compare the dubbing with moss and mix the colors as close as you can to the color of the moss.

Finally, take a **Black Blue Dun,** the dubbing of which is made from the fur of a black rabbit mixed with a little yellow. The wings are made from the feather of a blue pigeon's wing.

### *August*

For the month of August, Cotton tells us to use the flies from July.

To this, add another **Ant Fly,** made from the black-brown hair of a cow with some red wrap in the tag of the tail and a dark wings.

The next a fly is called the **Fern Fly.** Cotton instructs the angler to use the bracken fur of a hare's neck. Bracken refers to a fern which grows in open sunny places. It has black underground roots and its leaved are about five feet long. The roots of the bracken are filled with starch and were eaten by early peoples. It has been used in place of hopes in making beer.) The wings are made from the darkish-gray wing of a mallard's feather.

Next we have a **White Hackle** with a body of white mohair, wrapped about with a white hackled feather. This is assuredly taken for thistle down. We have also this month a **Harry Long Legs.** The body is made of bear's dun mixed with blue wool and wrapped all over with a brown hackle feather.

Lastly, take all the same browns and duns that were taken in May.

### *September.*

During September, take the same flies that were taken in April. To these Cotton adds only two flies: The **Camel-Brown Fly,** whipped about with red silk with dark gray mallard feathers for the wing, and a fly made of the black hair of a badger's skin, mixed with the softest yellow down of a sanded hog.

### *October, November, December*

In October, take the same flies that were taken in March. In November, use the same flies that were taken in February.

During December few men during Cotton's time angled with the fly. But if they do, Cotton suggests taking a **Brown Fly** that looks red in the hand but yellow when between your eye and the sun.

As you read and contemplate this list of fly patterns that is centuries old and review the colonial angler's tying techniques, I hope that you can see the evolution of our modern fly patterns. For this is part of an angler's quest to tie the properly dressed fly.

I will end this discourse on the colonial angler and its traditions with this quote from Izaak Walton:

*"And upon all that are lovers of virtue, and dare to trust in his providence, and be quiet, and go-a-angling."*

*The Colonial Angler's Manual of Flyfishing and Flytying*

# Appendix A: Trail of History

When you choose to re-create a person from history, you should seek out how he lived, where he lived, what kind of clothing he wore.... In general, you must find out everything you can about him.

   In this section, you will find lists of museums, book sellers, tackle makers, and additional readings. All of these people, places and things were instrumental in helping me to learn all I could about the colonial angler. Without their help, I never would have been able to portray "Ye Olde Colonial Angler of 1770" accurately.

## MUSEUMS

**The State Museum of Pennsylvania**, William Penn Memorial Building, Third and North Streets, PO Box 1026, Harrisburg, PA 17108–1026
The museum offers exciting collections and exhibits that explore Pennsylvania's rich history, culture, and natural hsitory.

**Daniel Boone Homestead,** RD2, Box 162, Birdsboro, PA 19508
The site of legendary pioneer Daniel Boone's birth in 1734 offers a unique glimpse of an early Pennsylvania settlement.

**Valley Forge National Historical Park,** National Park Service, Valley Forge, PA 19481
Site of the historic winter encampment of 1777–1778 where American Continental Soldiers survived hunger, disease and the winter's cold. During a recess of the Constitutional Convention in 1778, George Washington returned to Valley Forge and fished for trout in Valley Creek.

**Landis Valley Museum,** 2451 Kissel Hill Road, Lancaster, PA 17601
Experience rural life of southeastern Pennsylvania from colonial days through the 19th century.

**Johnson Hall,** Johnson Hall State Historic Site, Hall Avenue, Johnstown, NY 12095
Here in the southern foothills of the Adirondack Mountains of New York was the home of Sir William Johnson (1739–1774). He served as superintendent of Indian Affairs and was an avid sportsman and flyfisherman. The restored mansion will give visitors a glimpse of how an English Loyalist lived during the early 18th century.

**Catskill Fly Fishing Center and Museum,** RD1, Box 1300, Livingston Manor, NY 12758
Preserving the heritage, enhancing the present, protecting the future. The museum has displays of hundreds of flies, rods, reels and other artifacts from past and present masters of the art of flyfishing.

**Brandywine Battlefield,** Brandywine Battlefield Park, PO Box 202, Chadds Ford, PA 19317
Brandywine Battlefield is where Washington's troops battled the British in September 1777 for control of strategic terriotry near Philadelphia.

**American Museum of Fly Fishing,** PO Box 42, Manchester, VT 05254
An in-depth look at the history and traditions of flyfishing in our country.

**Philadelphia Maritime Museum,** 321 Chestnut St., Philadelphia, PA 19106
Maritime history of Pennsylvania and the nation is told through ship models, paintings and other artifacts.

**Colonial Williamsburg,** PO Box 1776, Williamsburg, VA 23187
The restored 18th-century Williamsburg offers visitors an exciting opportunity to see the city as it was prior to the American Revolution. It is a living, working colonial city, full of craftsmen, tradesmen, shop keepers and everyday folk demonstrating the way things were 200 years ago.

## BOOK SELLERS

**The Angler's Art,** P.O. Box 148, Plainfield, PA 17081.

**Judith Bowman Books,** Pound Ridge Road, Bedford, NY 10506.

**Raymond C. Rumpf & Son,** P.O. Box 319, Sellersville, PA 18960.
   (Also supplies quality flytying materials.)

**Rising Trout Sporting Books,** P.O. Box 338, Elmira, Canada N3B 2Z7.

**Sportsmen's Closet,** Bill Dromsky, 12 Main Street, Mainland, PA 19451.

## ANTIQUE AND COLLECTIBLE FISHING TACKLE

**Harold G. Herr (Doc),** 1190 West Main Street, Ephrata, PA 17522.

**Jack Mickievicz,** 8 Heather Lane, Douglassville, PA 19518.
(Also supplies quality flytying materials.)

## COLONIAL ANGLING TACKLE

**Ken Reinard,** 905 Hannah Drive, Lititz, PA 17543-9677.

## ADDITIONAL READING—Books

Bates, Jr. Joseph D. *The Art of the Atlantic Salmon Fly*. David B. Godine Publisher Inc. First edition, 1987.

Black, Adam and Charles. *A History of the Fish Hook*. English Language Edition, London. First edition, 1977.

Bottrall, Margaret. *Izaak Walton*. Longmans, Green and Co., London. First published in 1955.

Brooks, Joseph. *Trout Fishing*. Popular Science Publishing Co., Inc. 1972.

Caucci, Al and Nastasi, Bob. *Hatches*. Compora Hatch Ltd. 1975

Davy, Sir Humphrey. *Salmonia*. Freshet Press. 1971 edition.

Dawes, Mike. *The Flytyer's Manual*. Stoeger Publishing Co. 1986.

DuBois, Donald. *The Fisherman's Handbook of Trout Flies*. A.S. Barnes and Co., Inc. 1960.

Fox, Charles K. *Rising Trout*. Hawthorn Books, Inc. First edition, 1967.

Gabrielson, Iran. *The Fisherman's Encyclopedia*. Stackpole Books. 1950.

Gaidy, Charles. *Ephemeras*. First American edition, 1986.

Graumont, Radul and Wenstrom, Elmer. *Fisherman's Knots and Nets*. Cornell Maritime Press, New York. 1948.

Harris, J.R. *An Angler's Entomology*. A.S. Barnes and Co. 1973.

Henshall, James A. *Book of the Black Bass*. Bass Anglers Sportsman Society of America, Inc. 1978.

Hills, John Walker. *A History of Fly Fishing for Trout*. Freshet Press. 1971.

Jardine, Charles. *The Classic Guide to Fly-fishing for Trout*. Random House, New York. 1971.

Koller, Larry. *The Treasury of Angling*. Golden Press. 1963.

Leisenring, James. *The Art of Tying the Wet Fly and Fishing the Flymph*. Crown Publisher, New York. 1971.

Marbury, Mary Orvis. *Favorite Flies and Their Histories*. Charles T. Branford Co. Reprint edition, 1955.

McClane, A. J. *McClane's Standard Fishing Encyclopedia*. Holt, Rinehart and Winston. 1965.

McDonald, John. *Quill Gordon*. Alfred A. Knopf, Inc. 1972.

McNally's, Tom. *Tom McNally's Complete Book of Fishermen's Knots*. J. Philip O'Hara Inc. 1975.

Price, Taff. *Fly Patterns: An International Guide*. Exeter Books. 1986.

Ronalds, Alfred. *The Fly-fisher's Entomology*. The Wellfleet Press, London. Edition 1990.

Schullery, Paul. *American Fly Fishing: A History*. Nick Lyons Books. 1987.

Seccombe, Joseph. *A Discourse at Ammuskeeg-Falls in the Fishing Season*. Barre Publishers. 1971.

Shaw, Fred, G. *The Science of Fly Fishing for Trout*. Charles Scribner's Sons. First edition, 1925.

Southard, Charles Zibeon. *The Evolution of Trout and Trout Fishing in America*. E.P. Dutton and Co. 1928.

Tannatt, T.E. Pryce. *How to Dress Salmon Flies*. A & C Black Ltd. 1991 reprint.

Wright, Leonard M., Jr. *Fishing the Dry Fly as a Living Insect*. Nick Lyons Books. 1988.

## ADDITIONAL READING—Periodicals

"The Finer Points of Hook-making." Bramley, Alan. *Angler's Mail* 1993.

"Forging for Strength." Bamley, Alan. *Angler's Mail*. 1993.

"Doubles and Trebles." Bamley, Alan. *Angler's Mail*. 1993.

"Tempering and Testing." Bamley, Alan. *Angler's Mail.*1993.

"The Patron Saint of Angling." Brock, Paul, and Heaton, R.E. *This England.* Summer 1989.

"Are These Flies the Best Fish Getters?" Carhart, Arthur Hawthorne. *Outdoor Life.* December 1936.

"River Cane: Our American Bamboo." Massey, Jack. *Traditional Bow Hunter.* October/November 1993.

"Fish Hook Manufacturers." A.E. Partridge and Sons, Ltd. *Fly Tackle Dealer.* Winter 1986.

"Fishing Around Philadelphia." Vernon, Steven, K. *Pennsylvania Heritage.* Spring 1990.

"Collecting Old Fishing Books, Part One." Wetzel, Charles M. *Pennsylvania Angler.* March 1946.

"Collecting Old Fishing Books, Part Two." Wetzel, Charles M. *Pennsylvania Angler.* April 1946.

"Collecting Old Fishing Books, Part Three." Wetzel, Charles M. *Pennsylvania Angler.* May 1946.

"The Art of the Hook." Cameron, Kenneth. *Trout.* Spring 1977.

# Appendix B: Bibliography

Barker, Thomas. *The Art of Angling.* London, 1653.

Berners, Dame Juliana. *A Treatyse of Fysshynge with an Angle.* Westminster, Wynkyn de Worde. 1496.

Berners, Dame Juliana. *A Treatise on Fishing with a Hook.* Rendered into modern English by William Van Wyck, North River Press Inc. 1979.

Dennys, John. *The Secrets of Angling.* Freshet Press edition, 1970.

Popkin, Susan A. and Allen, Roger B. *Gone Fishing: A History of Fishing in River, Bay and Sea.* Philadelphia Maritime Museum, Philadelphia, Pennsylvania. 1987.

Walton, Izaak and Charles Cotton. *The Compleat Angler.* Bethune edition, John Wiley and Sons, 1880.

# Appendix C: Acknowledgements

A successful project has never prospered without the help of dedicated individuals. The following is a list of The Colonial Angler's *Fidus Achates,* his faithful friends. Each person has contributed to this project in a special way.

Gillies to The Angler. A special thank you to each one of them for taking their time to help me present colonial angling in the proper manner: Eric Reinard, Gary Myers, Brian Reedy, Dan Fisher, Vince Newcomer, Marc Brier, and Larry Spittler.

To the friends who made the clothing to properly attire The Colonial Angler: Tidy's Storehouse, Ken and Dianne Tidy; Ephrata Shoe Co., Inc., Dan Mentzer; F&M Hat Company Inc., Robert Fichthorn; and Rita Spittler.

To the photographers who used their talent to document The Angler's tackle, methods, and adventures: John Bergeuin, Bob Highley, Joe Endy, Dan Fisher, Rita Spittler, Paul Ahnert, Jack Hubly, and Dolores "Dolly" Leed. Dave Ihde: pages 44, 45, 46, 49, 50, 52. 53, 58, 59, 61, 62, 63, 72, 73–90. John Shuman: pages 4, 11, 12 , 28, 29, 30, 31, 32, 38, 39, 43, 51, 52, 56, 57, 62, 63. 67, 70, 71, Lee Kerschner.

To the German Regiment, especially Cary Shaner, Rick Edwards, Jere Brubaker, and the Grundsau!

A special thank you to Jack Mickievicz and Harold G. Herr (Doc). Both are specialists in antique fishing tackle and allowed me to conduct research with them and utilize their private libraries and collections of antique tackle. They also helped me to keep on track and in tune with our angling heritage.

The art of hook making: O. Mustad & Son, Inc., Skip Mortenson, and Partridge of Redditch, Alan Bramley.

To George Darby, for the use of his antique tackle.

To John Miller, for his knowledge of tempering wire for hooks.

To my editor Ayleen Stellhorn who used her time and talent to patiently read my ideas and put them into a readable discourse for all to enjoy.

To Alan Giagnocavo, the publisher of Fox Chapel Books, who had the idea to bring this book to life.

To Colonial Williamsburg for allowing me to portray the Colonial Angler during their Publick Times, and to Baxter Hartinge and Bill White.

To a proper gentleman from North Carolina, Jim Daniel.

To all who help promote The Colonial Angler, especially: Barry and Gerry Serviente, Chuck Furimski, Jim Merritt, Carl McCardell, Mike O'Brien, Jerry Stercho.

To all my friends and angling companions who have shared their knowledge with me in the days afield enjoying the sport of angling.

To Joe Endy, who ties flies with synthetic materials. A most ingenious flyfisherman.

**And to my father, Irven S. Reinard ("Peps") for his blacksmithing skills, and for first taking me fishing.**

And to Him who made it all possible.

# *Index*